W9-DBY-255

The Old Guide's Secret
CALENDAR OF
FISH ACTIVITY

Seasonal Rhythm and Response

by the In-Fisherman Staff

Published by
In-Fisherman®

The In-Fisherman Secrets Series

Corporate Director	*Al Lindner*
Publisher Emeritus	*Ron Lindner*
Chief Executive Officer/Publisher	*Stuart Legaard*
Chief Operations Officer	*Dan Sura*
Chief Financial Officer	*Gary McEnelly*

Editor In Chief	*Doug Stange*
Editor	*Dave Csanda*
Editor	*Steve Quinn*
Editor	*Matt Straw*
Managing Editor	*Joann Phipps*
Photo Editor/Design	*Jan Couch*
Associate Editor	*Eileen Firkus*
Production Assistant	*Scott Lawrence*
Designer/Illustrator	*Jim Pfaff*
Production Manager	*Scott Pederson*

THE OLD GUIDE'S SECRET
CALENDAR OF FISH ACTIVITY

Compiled by	*Doug Stange and Steve Quinn with the In-Fisherman Staff*
Edited by	*Doug Stange, Steve Quinn, and Joann Phipps*
Layout and Design by	*Jim Pfaff with Jan Couch*
Species Illustration by	*Joe Tomelleri*
Litho Prep and Printing by	*Bang Printing*

ISBN 0-929384-68-7

The In-Fisherman Secrets Series

An

F (Fish) + L (Location) + P (Presentation) = S (Success)™

Educational Service

visit our Web site: www.in-fisherman.com

Printing Edition
10 9 8 7 6

TABLE OF CONTENTS

INTRODUCTION

No creature is less affected by seasonal changes in the environment than humans. We may feel cheerful on a warm spring day or down after a week of rain; we dress light when it's sultry and cover up when it's cold. But our metabolism remains constant. We eat three meals a day, go to work, raise children, and sleep on a similar schedule year round.

Scientists call us homeotherms, creatures with stable body temperature, regardless of the outside environment. Other mammals and birds also are homeothermic (often called warm-blooded), but many species migrate or hibernate, eat less, or grow extra fur during cold seasons. Nearly all animals also mate, give birth, and raise young during precise time frames that allow adults to eat heavily and feed their young when forage is most abundant. We don't feel these constraints since our food supply depends on the local supermarket.

Seasonal and even daily changes in weather and water temperature affect fish far more than they affect birds and mammals. Their feeding activity, digestion, metabolism, and growth rate are influenced by season and water temperature, in accordance with their genetic makeup. Angling success depends to a large extent upon understanding seasonal activity of various fish species.

As a result, Al and Ron Lindner developed the concept of Calendar Periods before they published the first issue of *In-Fisherman* magazine. They had used this concept in their early days of guiding and promoting fishing tackle, and it worked like magic. Indeed, they termed their traveling fishing show, which often produced fish on bodies of water where local anglers weren't catching any, their "magic act."

Ron and Al, who learned to fish in natural lakes in the northern United States, became particularly interested in how seasonal changes affect fish behavior and determine successful angling techniques. Seasonal changes are most dramatic in the North where water temperatures range from around 80°F in the heat of summer to 32°F for several months of winter. Yet more subtle and gradual changes that occur in southern waters and even in the tropics also profoundly affect fish behavior.

The In-Fisherman Calendar includes 10 Periods in an annual cycle. Dividing the annual continuum into 10 periods is somewhat arbitrary; indeed, the periods merge at their boundaries. The 10 time frames, however, focus attention on subtleties in water conditions and fish response. The In-Fisherman Calendar Periods don't follow the 12-month Gregorian calendar, since fish have no regard for such artificial schemes. Anglers who adhere too closely to our 12-month calendar miss key changes in fish behavior.

The Lindners based the original In-Fisherman Calendar of Fish Activity on the behavior of fish in lakes and reservoirs. Many of the same seasonal trends occur in rivers, with the exceptions of the Turnover Period and the Frozen Water Period. Other periods like the Summer Peak and Postsummer occur in rivers, though their timing may differ from periods in nearby lakes. The reactions of fish are different, too, since fish in rivers tend to migrate much farther after spawning and before winter.

Doug Stange
Editor In Chief

CALENDAR PERIODS DEFINED

A Vest-Pocket Guide to Understanding Each of the 10 Calendar Periods of Fish Response

Coldwater Period (Spring)

Where waters freeze, the spring Coldwater Period begins at ice-out, lasting until the Prespawn Period begins. In natural lakes, this period can bring fast fishing for panfish that enter shallow bays to eat plankton that quickly blooms in the spring sun or invertebrates that creep from the mud to eat detritus.

Huge schools of minnows also appear to feed, drawing pike, largemouth bass, and sometimes walleyes. On warm sunny days, bluegills, crappies, and bass hold near decayed weeds or shoreline cover like fallen trees and beaver lodges, moving deeper during cloudy or windy conditions and at dusk. Walleyes and pike tend to hold deeper during the day, moving inshore at dusk for a quick bite.

Fish are concentrated but tend to be spooky in clear shallow water. Light line, long casts, small baits, and patient presentations work best. Floats suspend light jigs and livebaits, and they allow fish to casually approach or anglers to drift offerings across small bays.

In reservoirs that don't freeze, fish tend to hold deeper until waters warm into the low 50°F range. Bass and crappies hold in large groups along edges of creek channels to feed on threadfin shad. Predators and prey typically hold in depths from 12 to 20 feet.

The length of this period for each fish species depends on spring warming trends that send walleyes directly to spawning areas and move black bass toward prespawn locations. The Coldwater Period in spring can last for several weeks in southern waters and usually a couple weeks or less in northern lakes.

Prespawn Period

Prespawn marks the start of spawning activities that produce a new year class of fish. The Prespawn Period begins when fish begin moving toward spawning areas, such as a run of walleyes up a river or northern pike moving under an ice-covered lake toward a spawning marsh, or when largemouth bass move to shallower water to feed prior to spawning. Examples of prespawn movement are crappies moving into a lily pad bay shortly after ice-out and catfish moving upstream as a river warms toward the 60°F range. In one case, spawning is imminent. In the other, fish may move from the initial concentration area before spawning takes place.

Fish usually are concentrated during prespawn, since adult fish in one part of a body of water react similarly when water warms or run-off increases. Spawning areas or prespawn staging areas usually represent a tiny fraction of the habitat available to fish, so concentrations are heavy at times. This usually means good fishing

The Ten In-Fisherman Calendar Periods

1 Prespawn	2 Spawn	3 Postspawn	4 Presummer	5 Summer Peak	6 Summer	7 Postsummer	8 Turnover	9 Coldwater	10 Winter

Pike in a Central Michigan Natural Lake

1	2	3	4	5	6	7	8	9	10

Pike in a Northern Saskatchewan Lake

1	2	3	4	5	6	7	8	9	10

*The 10 In-Fisherman Calendar Periods were devised to identify yearly periods of fish activity. For comparison, **Chart 1** shows the periods as equal, which is almost never the case. **Chart 2** shows the approximate length of the 10 periods for pike in a central Michigan natural lake. **Chart 3** shows the periods for pike in a northern Saskatchewan lake. Saskatchewan's cold climate extends the Coldwater Period and condenses the other nine Calendar Periods.*

While Calendar Periods always occur in order, their length varies for each species based on geographical location and body of water type. The periods are not the same for each species. Largemouth bass, for example, often are in their Spawn Period when pike are in their Presummer or Summer Peak Period.

Calendar Periods help pinpoint fish location and activity level.

Catfish like this channel cat go through an extended Prespawn Period that results in extended good fishing.

for anglers who locate fish, though the willingness of individual fish to bite may vary from poor for prespawn pike or muskies; to fair for walleyes, American shad or steelhead; to positive but cautious for crappies and sunfish; to nearly ravenous for largemouth bass and channel catfish.

The Prespawn Period ends when fish spawn. The length of this period varies among species. Northern pike may swim into a marsh, spawn, and leave within a week. Fall-run steelhead, on the other hand, make a prespawn migration upriver in fall and spend the winter there before spawning when water temperatures reach the 40°F range.

The length of this period also depends on latitude and how quickly waters warm. In southern reservoirs, prespawn for largemouth bass may last 10 weeks, while in the northern United States and Canada, three weeks is typical. The length of the Prespawn Period also depends on seasonal weather. Spring weather that warms fast shortens the prespawn period, while a series of cold fronts prolong it.

Large bodies of water have bays, creek arms, or river systems that warm at different rates. Prespawn can begin weeks earlier in one area, and fish in different parts of the lake or reservoir may be in various Calendar Periods. Identifying the Calendar Period correctly and matching typical fish behavior dramatically improves fishing success.

Spawn Period

The Spawn Period encompasses activities directly related to spawning. For fish like walleyes, yellow perch, or striped bass, the spawn is brief. Females deposit all their eggs and quickly leave the spawning area. Since male fish often try to fertilize the eggs of several females, they remain on spawning grounds until the last female departs.

Fish that provide parental care have a much longer spawning period. Male bluegills, bass, and other members of the sunfish family build nests, lure females, fertilize eggs, and guard eggs and fry until young fish are independent. In northern

9

climates, the Spawn Period for male nest builders may last four to six weeks, a week or less for females.

Spawning fish usually are preoccupied with a series of species-specific behaviors that lead to successful fertilization. Sometimes they refuse to bite natural baits or artificials. At other times, however, they strike instinctively or in defense of their nest. Some species like bluegills take baits presented near nesting colonies. The large average size of spawning fish offers some of the best fishing of the year.

Postspawn Period

After spawning activities cease, fish generally move from spawning sites to areas that offer better feeding opportunities. The shift may be gradual or abrupt, depending on species of fish, available cover, prey location, and weather and water conditions. Some fish species begin eating heavily soon after spawning while others seem to undergo a period of recuperation. Indeed, fish that defend young, like sunfish and catfish, may have torn fins, lacerations, and be in poor condition. Some die, others begin the recuperation process by eating. The combination of shifting locations, sparse cover, and lower feeding levels often make fishing during the Postspawn Period unpredictable.

Presummer Period

Presummer is another transitional phase as fish begin establishing home ranges and daily feeding patterns that may eventually last throughout summer. Aquatic plants flourish, offering increasing cover in shallow areas and out to the deepest water sunlight penetrates enough to grow plants. Weedgrowth, though, isn't so dense as later in summer. Water temperatures during this phase typically run in the 60°F range, though they may be 10 degrees lower or higher for some species in some regions. Water typically hasn't stratified.

Fish Activity Level   *Walleyes in a Central Minnesota Lake*

* very active   M = Male
+ active   F = Female
○ medium
□ slow

	VERNAL EQUINOX	ICE-OUT SOLSTICE			SUMMER EQUINOX
JAN.	FEB.	MAR.	APR.	MAY	JUN

| Frozen Water □ to ○ | ○ Coldwater | Prespawn + | Spawn + M □ F | Post-spawn + M □ F | Presummer + | S Pe * |

| Periods Determined Primarily by Water Temperature | Periods Determined Primarily by Fish Behavior | |

10

When weather is exceptionally warm in late spring, the Presummer Period passes quickly to the Summer Peak Period. During cool, cloudy springs, however, the transition may take several weeks. Fishing often is spotty because lakewide patterns haven't developed. Now is the time to experiment with a variety of lure types, retrieves, and colors.

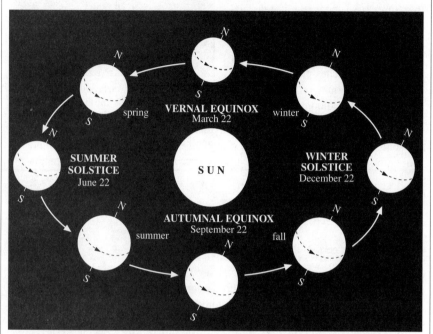

Spring, summer, fall, winter. The pendulum swings between seasons, bringing evident changes on land, but more difficult-to-define changes underwater. Studies show that photoperiod (length of daylight) influences the tempo of the environment, from microorganisms to top-of-the-line predators. The intensity and duration of light in a yearly cycle influences migrations, spawning, and feeding.

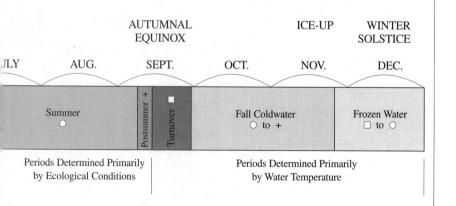

Summer Peak Period

The Summer Peak usually begins after the first hot spell during late spring or early summer. Water temperatures rise near their seasonal highs, and lakes and reservoirs seem to become alive. Newly hatched fish swarm the shallows and open water where insect hatches produce feeding binges at all hours of the day and night. Plankton blooms give lakes a greenish hue and produce better fishing for all species under bright conditions. Zooplankton multiply on their diet of phytoplankton, establishing a food chain based on these tiny animals and directly feeding omnivorous gamefish like bluegills, crappies, and perch.

During this period that may last only one to two weeks, predators, including black bass, northern pike, and walleye, feed heavily, often in relatively shallow water. Fishing at dawn and dusk and during rain showers is particularly good, but the middle of the day also can be productive, due to the elevated level of the food chain.

Summer Period

Summer is the longest Calendar Period throughout most of the United States, lasting 8 to 10 weeks in the northern U.S. and southern Canada and up to four months in southern waters. Most of a fish's annual growth occurs during this period, so feeding is heavy. In some regions, however, where summer temperatures exceed the optimal range for a species, temporary lags in feeding activity and growth may occur. A hot spell in Kansas may put reservoir

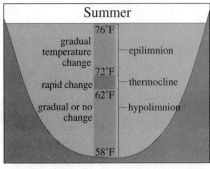

The upper layer (warmwater) may be from 12 to 40 feet thick, while the thermocline may be 2 to 15 feet thick. The lower level (coldwater) usually contains less dissolved oxygen than the upper layer.

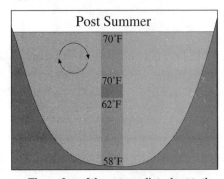

The surface of the water radiates heat to the atmosphere at night, as water above the thermocline gradually cools. The thermocline remains intact but is close in temperature to the layer above. Oxygen-poor water remains trapped below.

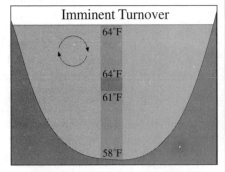

The thermocline shrinks as it approaches the same temperature as the uniform mass of water above.

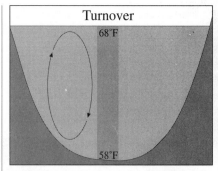

Turnover

68°F

58°F

The thermocline disintegrates and water mixes from surface to bottom. The water continues to cool as it circulates, aided by wind. The oxygen level of the water drops for a short time as the oxygen-depleted hypolimnion mixes with the water above.

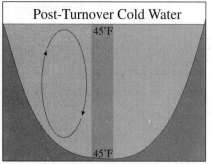

Post-Turnover Cold Water

45°F

45°F

Temperature is uniform. Wind action circulates and oxygenates water, which is a uniform temperature.

walleyes off feed, for example, and similar though hotter conditions in a Florida lake can limit largemouth bass to feeding at night.

Fish generally move deeper to find cooler water. Productive depth zones typically are deeper than during the Summer Peak. Bluegills may hold on bars at 20 feet, and pike and muskies may suspend over deep open water. Maximum depth often is limited by the thermocline that forms in most lakes and reservoirs during summer, because water below the thermocline is too cold for warmwater species and oxygen content is too low in all but oligotrophic or early-stage mesotrophic waters. In most lakes, the thermocline occurs between 20 and 35 feet, shifting somewhat with air temperature, wind, current, and rainfall. In older reservoirs with abundant organic matter on the bottom, the thermocline can be as shallow as 10 feet. Reeling in a dead minnow is a sure sign you're fishing too deep.

During the Summer Period, fish develop feeding patterns that can yield good catches once anglers define the pattern. Cold fronts, storms, or shifts in wind direction can alter patterns. And patterns sometimes change for no obvious reason.

Postsummer Period

When night temperatures dip to their lowest in months, the Postsummer Period arrives. Daytime temperatures on a hot sunny day may still reach 90°F, but water temperatures decline due to cooler nights. Panfish and predatory gamefish feed in deep and shallow cover. On calm days and evenings, bass and muskies may feed heavily on the surface if perch, bluegill, or other preyfish move toward the surface to feed on insect hatches.

Some aquatic plants like the broad leaf pondweed (cabbage) turn brown, no longer holding fish as they did during the Summer Period. Cold-resistant plant species like coontail thicken and grow deeper as waters cool. Fishing patterns are more volatile than in summer, but huge catches are possible.

Turnover Period

Fall weather cools surface water, making it heavy enough to mix with cooler water in the upper part of the thermocline. Wind furthers the mixing, as the thermocline narrows and finally disintegrates. As water mixes from surface to bottom, it may darken due to rising bottom sediments. Hydrogen sulfide and other gases trapped on the bottom are released and may produce a musky or sulfur odor. On sonar, pieces of broken weeds can be seen floating at mid-depths.

Turnover produces unpredictable fishing because productive patterns suddenly fail as cover, water color, temperature, and oxygen profiles change rapidly. We don't know whether this change causes fish to feed less actively following this change or if they feed where anglers don't fish. The typical turnover slump probably stems from a combination of these factors.

Effects of turnover on fishing usually last only a few days on a particular lake or reservoir, and the timing of turnover can vary over several weeks within a region. Windswept shallow lakes with dark water turn over earlier than clear protected lakes.

Coldwater Period

When water temperatures stabilize in the low 50°F range following turnover, the fall Coldwater Period begins. This period continues until waters freeze or reach their annual lows. In the far north, however, this period may last only a month or so if winter comes early.

The Coldwater Period is noted for producing big fish, particularly largemouth bass, walleye, northern pike, and muskie. Large fish seem to feed heavily before the onset of winter, yet few anglers fish at this time. Cold water allows coolwater predators like pike, muskies, and walleyes to roam shallow or hold deep, depending on the local species of preyfish and their abundance.

Thinning weedgrowth concentrates largemouth bass on remaining green weeds or among shallow emergent plants. Panfish like crappies and sunfish shift deeper as minnows and zooplankton evacuate shallow shoreline areas where water temperatures fluctuate considerably.

As water temperatures drop into the low 40°F range, fish activity slows and fishing becomes uncomfortable on all but the mildest late-fall days. Once the surface temperature is 39°F or less, a calm, cold night can ice over a lake or bay. Walleyes, pike, and crappies often move to winter spots before waters freeze.

Anglers generally agree that the Coldwater Period means fine fishing once consolidated groups are found.

Most fish are at least somewhat active under ice. Big pike, however, thrive in cold water. Winter means continued activity that usually means good fishing.

Winter or Frozen Water Period

Millions of dedicated ice anglers rejoice when enough ice forms to support their weight, then the weight of a snowmobile, and finally a truck. Early-ice often produces excellent fishing for walleyes, big pike, and panfish. Largemouth bass bite with some regularity once their located. Smallmouths are less catchable, and catfish become dormant.

In many waters, preferred depths range from less than 10 feet for pike and chain pickerel to over 30 feet for walleyes. Yellow perch hug bottom, while sunfish usually suspend a few feet higher, and crappies still higher. Rainbow and brook trout often cruise just below the ice.

Scientific studies suggest that most species seldom feed under the ice but can be caught with smaller and more subtle presentations than those used for open water. Light line, livebait, subtle bait movements, close attention to depthfinder readings, and staying warm usually are keys to success.

Note that walleyes may begin prespawn movements while ice covers parts of a lake. And pike may enter marshes to spawn while a lake or reservoir remains ice covered.

Lakes, ponds, and reservoirs in the southern third of the United States rarely or never freeze, so the Coldwater Period is extended through the time waters remain near their annual minimums. Some species—crappies, stripers, hybrid stripers, and black bass in some situations—provide good fishing through the Winter Period.

Having gained a basic understanding of the 10 Calendar Periods, we'll look more closely at seven of the most popular gamefish species across the country for secrets to consistent catches.

YEAR OF THE NORTHERN PIKE

Secrets to Seasonal Periods of Response

The northern pike is the coolest of North American coolwater game-fish. They inhabit lakes, rivers, and reservoirs from Alaska to as far south as Missouri. The pike's fierce appearance and aggressive nature have contributed to many tall tales over the centuries and continue to fuel the imagination of anglers. Northern pike apparently require a period of ice cover or frigid conditions for egg production and maturation. Although stocked pike have grown large in states as far south as Georgia (18-pound 2-ounce state record), spawning doesn't occur. Agencies in southern states have stopped stocking pike because waters are too warm for ideal growth, expensive culture operations are necessary to maintain fisheries, predation on other native or naturalized species may be a problem, and anglers haven't shown enough interest. In their native range, however, pike are popular trophy fish, and smaller specimens provide fast fishing and good eating.

Pike also inhabit waters in the northern latitudes of Europe and Asia, where they've grown even larger than in North America. Arno Wilhelm caught the largest recorded pike, 67 pounds 33¾ ounces, from a flooded pit in Germany.

Coldwater Period (Spring)

Water Temperature: Warming Slightly from Annual Minimum
General Fish Mood: Neutral to Positive

In most areas, pike begin prespawn movements while ice remains on lakes or reservoirs. In some cases, however, there's a short transition period once ice begins to break up or has left waters in the southern part of the pike's range. And in rivers, pike may hold outside spawning bays after ice has drifted downstream.

In these situations, anglers can take numbers of big pike as well as many small ones. Pike often can be spotted as they hold among old bulrushes or stalks of dead plants. Casting and retrieving lures past their snouts often is more than their predatory instinct can stand. They'll bust minnow baits, in-line spinners, spinnerbaits, spoons, and flies, particularly on warm sunny days. At other times, deadbaits on quick-strike rigs work best. The Spring Coldwater Period ends as pike enter spawning areas, which may be near or far from where they staged.

Pike Calendar

1. Prespawn	4. Presummer	7. Postsummer	10. Winter*
2. Spawn	5. Summer Peak	8. Fall Turnover	
3. Postspawn	6. Summer	9. Coldwater	

*Coldest water of the year.

Calendar Periods Equal	1	2	3	4	5	6	7	8	9	10
Pike	1 2	3	4		5	6	7	8	9	10

Prespawn Period

Water Temperature: 32°F to 42°F
(from just before ice-out to ice-out)
General Fish Mood: Neutral

During late winter when ice still covers lakes, pike gradually leave offshore bars and sunken islands and concentrate in shallower shoreline areas—points and bars near shallow coves and marshes where they'll spawn. The journey can be short in small lakes or many miles in large river systems, connecting lakes, or the Great Lakes. Pike have been known to move 30 miles or more to a spawning site.

Cues that trigger this locational shift aren't clear. Water temperature remains constant under ice cover, so temperature doesn't appear to trigger the movement. Lengthening daylight has been proposed as a motivating force. Yet timing of prespawn movements varies from year to year and can be altered by local weather conditions.

While pike aren't focused on feeding during the Prespawn Period, they readily take deadbait and strike slowly retrieved lures, especially in the earlier phases of

18

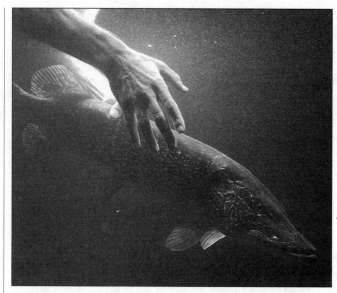

Big pike are particularly vulnerable to fishing pressure and should be released to sustain good fishing. Pike release is most successful during periods of cold or cool water temperatures.

the Prespawn Period. Males typically are more aggressive; consequently, more males are caught than females. Both sexes, while not aggressive, are concentrated, so expect action once you locate fish. This is especially true in Canadian wilderness waters.

Channels between lakes and those that connect lakes to marshes lose ice cover first, particularly if current is present. Pike often move into smaller, weedier lakes or marshes to spawn. Warmer inflowing water provides a beacon that pike rarely ignore.

Spawn Period

Water Temperature: 39°F to 52°F
General Fish Mood: Negative

Triggers that probably include length of daylight, current, water temperature, and resulting physiological changes push pike into spawning habitat. Most fish move into spawning marshes at night and over a period of 10 days to two weeks. Males enter earlier and in greater numbers than larger females. Once in the spawning area, pike apparently wait a few days before spawning.

Two or more males typically swim close to a large female, and the group rolls in unison, simultaneously emitting eggs and sperm over shallow weeds. The eggs, which measure less than 1/8 inch in diameter, stick to vegetation and twigs. The same group of fish may swim a short distance, then spawn again. Some fish may leave the group and others join. This behavior is called "scooting" because large fish often produce wakes as they move quickly in shallow water.

The peak spawning temperature ranges from 39°F to 46°F. Pike may begin spawning at temperatures as low as 39°F and as high as the low 50°F range. So temperature isn't the only factor. Other environmental conditions—weather and light intensity—also have an effect.

Pike generally release eggs and sperm within a couple days. If the spawning area is shallow, most adult pike soon leave. Since many spawning areas hold few forage fish at this time of year, the need to feed may push pike into shallower areas of the main lake or river, but near the spawning site. If the area provides adequate depth (2 to 5 feet), some smaller pike may remain for several months. But warm water and dense weedgrowth eventually push them out.

Remember, while actual spawning is taking place in one area, in other areas, groups of pike may be waiting to spawn, and in still others, the spawn may be completed. The Spawn Period must therefore be considered a local activity. Yet within most bodies of water, most pike spawn during a two-week period or less. In large reservoirs or the Great Lakes, however, spawning may last a bit longer.

Most fish arrive at a spawn site between dusk and midnight. Yet even though they arrive at night, spawning usually takes place during daylight, often in early afternoon. Calm, sunny days seem to be preferred.

Postspawn Period

Water Temperature: High 40°F Range to Low 50°F Range
General Fish Mood: Neutral to Positive

Water temperatures in the mid-50°F range are typical during the Postspawn Period, which usually lasts a week or two until pike recuperate and shift into Presummer Period patterns. Postspawn pike don't show much of a slump in feeding activity. Cool water, shallow cover, and abundant prey provide the potential for good pike fishing. Sunfish and crappies may also be shallow, and yellow perch may be spawning in nearby weedbeds. In oligotrophic lakes, however, large pike may quickly move from spawning areas to open water where they feed on ciscoes, not returning until the following spring.

Productive cover for pike primarily consists of emerging lily pads and new growth of cabbage, milfoil, cabomba, and other species of submerged aquatic plants. Bulrushes offer cover on harder bottoms, and large pike may hold near boulders on shallow flats or along breaklines in lakes and rivers.

In waters where spawning bays are considerably separated from feeding areas, Postspawn brings inconsistent fishing. Pike may be biting one day and gone the next. Visualize the route back to the main lake or reservoir, or to a summer holding area, to determine areas where pike will hold. By this time, however, pike are beginning to cross over that thin line distinguishing the Postspawn Period from the Presummer Period.

Presummer Period

Water Temperature: Mid 50°F to Low 60°F Range
General Fish Mood: Neutral to Positive

While the Postspawn Period is characterized as a resting stage during which fish scatter and resume feeding, a change is imminent. Presummer is a time of emerging weedgrowth and developing food chains. Pike need nourishment, and the resumption of regular feeding indicates the beginning of the Presummer Period.

A Guide To The Calendar Periods for Pike

Period	Description	Key Factors
Prespawn	Length varies between lakes, rivers, or reservoirs. Main movement toward spawning areas.	Ice Melt. Water temperature. Hormone level. Length of daylight. Bottom conditions.
Spawn	Very short period. But all spawning does not take place at the same time. Fishing is poor.	Water temperature. Hormone level. Bottom condition.
Postspawn	Recuperation period for females. Males may be more aggressive, but fishing usually is slow.	Dispersal from spawning areas.
Presummer	Peak movement for all sizes of pike. Pike are actively feeding. Many fishing patterns.	Water temperature. Food chain.
Summer Peak	Pike niches form for summer. Smaller fish in shallow water are active. Larger pike become more difficult to locate.	Food chain. Prey size. Water temperature.
Summer	The bulk of the fishing season for most anglers. Niches remain separate. Natural food chain is at its peak.	Food chain and weedgrowth fully developed. Oxygen becomes a factor. Water temperature.
Postsummer	Water begins cooling rapidly. Different niches meld as pike switch locations. Pike activity increases as the water temperature drops to 65°F.	Food chain slows. Water Temperature.
Turnover	A classic situation on bodies of water that stratify during summer. Surface water cools and sinks. A general mixing of the water.	Oxygen. Mixing water. Water Temperature.
Coldwater	Excellent time for trophy pike. Good movements.	Location of prey.
Winter	Long period. Pike continue feeding. Fishing can be good.	Location of prey including deadbait.

While no absolute temperature indicates when pike enter the Presummer Period, surface water temperatures rising into the high 50°F or low 60°F range indicate that this phase is underway and pike will be biting. Note, however, that pike of different sizes behave differently, depending on water quality and available prey.

For example, big females that returned to open water during the postspawn dispersal continue to function in these zones, but they begin to feed more regularly. Intermediate-size pike may not move deep until surface water warms into the upper

Big pike prefer cold or cool water and often descend to the thermocline level during summer as surface temperatures rise.

60°F range. Look for pike from 3 to 10 pounds on shoreline points near fast drop-offs, relating to various food sources. Small pike remain shallow most of the year, relating to weedy flats and the shiners and small panfish that live there.

Pike can be difficult to pinpoint during the Presummer Period as patterns change with increasing weedgrowth, rising temperatures, and shifting prey locations. It's possible to catch several pike by rigging livebait in deep water, several more while trolling mid-depth flats, and some more by casting spoons to shallow water.

Most lunker pike taken between the Spawn and Postsummer periods are caught during the Presummer Period. Small and medium-size pike increase activity levels as the Summer Peak Period approaches.

Pike feed primarily during daylight. Expect peaks of activity in the morning and evening. Dark, overcast days with a chop on the water can also be excellent.

Slowly, as surface water temperatures climb, pike of all sizes move to the niches they'll occupy for the next two Calendar Periods. They also begin targeting specific prey—those most available within their environmental niches.

The Presummer Period is a time of transition when surface waters transform a body of water from the cooler environment of spring to the warmer environment of summer. Fish begin regrouping, primarily by size, and consistent fishing patterns emerge.

Summer Peak Period

Water Temperature: *Mid 60°F Range to Low 70°F Range*
General Fish Mood: *Positive*

As the summer solstice approaches, the Presummer Period shifts into the Summer Peak, a short period of excellent fishing for small- and intermediate-size pike (fish up to 12 pounds or so on the best waters). A span of relatively calm hot weather triggers this bite. In many cases, this is the first hot weather of the season, and more importantly, the first hot nights. It's also a time when large and trophy-size pike seem to disappear.

Most of a lake's ecosystem reaches its maximum production during this period. All species except catfish have completed spawning. Insect species hatch. Rooted aquatic plants produce lush weedlines, and fishing is generally excellent for walleyes and bass.

Lunker pike must find cool refuges with sufficient prey to satisfy their needs. Smaller pike tolerate water in the upper 70°F range, while intermediate-size pike avoid water above 70°F. Various sizes of pike usually segregate for the duration of summer because of these temperature preferences. Anglers must tailor their fishing to the size fish they want to catch and catch rates that satisfy them. Anglers who target giant pike during summer in pressured waters should be satisfied with a fish every two weeks, while 20 pike from one to four pounds isn't unusual in a day of spinnerbaiting the flats.

Summer Period

Water Temperature: *Maximum Temperatures of the Year*
General Fish Mood: *Neutral to Positive*

The Romans believed the dog star Sirius rose with the sun, giving the days of July and August a double measure of heat, thus the term "dog days." While a misnomer that implies lethargy for most other species of gamefish, the term is appropriate for big pike. With water temperatures at their annual maximum, big pike conserve energy in deep cool water, feeding only at optimal times.

Lakes, rivers, and reservoirs bloom with food, and predators become more selective in their feeding. Stratification and the associated loss of oxygen in the deepest layers of mesotrophic and eutrophic lakes, intense sunlight, boating activity, and fishing pressure affect the behavior of pike.

Summer fishing can be perplexing. Feeding periods may be short and unpredictable, even for small or medium-size pike. Savvy anglers seek big pike in pockets of cold water near springs, cool tributaries, or thermal upwellings. An electronic temperature gauge with a probe on a long wire is essential. On waters without cool sanctuaries, large pike seem to reduce their metabolism and may lose weight until cooling water revives them.

Postsummer Period

Water Temperature: *Cooling From the Annual Maximum*
General Fish Mood: *Neutral to Positive*

Consider the Postsummer Period a reversal of the Presummer Period. It's a time when bodies of water shift from a warmer to a cooler environment. At the end of summer, warm days often are followed by cool nights that gradually reduce water temperatures. Shorter daylight hours seem to signal the ecosystem to slow the pace of life.

Most of the annual food production in lakes, rivers, and reservoirs has been completed, and summer's time of plenty gives way to reduced food stocks. The density of aquatic plants also begins to decline. Insect hatches dwindle, and in some systems, water levels fall. Preyfish also shift position as they grow in size but decrease in numbers, and as cover diminishes.

In most waters, good pike fishing, especially for trophy pike, occurs during the Postsummer Period as water temperatures decline into the mid and low 60°F range. In mesotrophic waters, big pike that may have sought coolwater refuges during summer now can forage in shallow areas or suspend in open water. Small pike scatter.

In cold oligotrophic waters that through the seasons provide food at various depths, pike may remain in deep water. But if the prey base is perch, panfish, bullheads, and walleyes, expect pike of all sizes to move shallower, following their prey.

In contrast to the Summer Period, pike now tend to hold in feeding locations for extended periods—weeks if dramatic weather changes don't occur. Gradual change is typical as water temperatures decline and stratification begins to erode.

Turnover Period

Water Temperature: *Upper 50°F to Low 50°F Range*
General Fish Mood: *Negative*

Cool-running rivers may produce good fishing all season. Rivers usually don't turn over.

Thermal and chemical stratification disintegrates in fall turnover. Rivers, shallow windswept lakes and reservoirs, or impoundments with substantial flow don't stratify and don't turn over. Fish in these waters are not subject to the sudden environmental changes that accompany turnover.

Lakes and reservoirs that turn over remain stratified through the Summer and Postsummer periods. Then the sun grows less direct, and seasonal hard, driving, cold winds and rain begin chilling the surface temperature of the water, mixing it with the upper layer of the thermocline. Within a day or two, waters from surface to bottom mix and equalize in temperature, dissolved oxygen, and pH. At times, stagnant bottom water releases a sulfurous odor as it rises to the surface. Dead weeds and other bottom debris may float on the surface, appear on sonar at mid-depths, or wash ashore.

Pike move deep or shallow as structural features, cover, and preyfish lead them. Fishing activity typically slows until waters clear and fish settle into new patterns. Fishing during the Turnover Period is difficult. But since all bodies of water don't turn over at the same time, switch to waters that have already turned over, haven't yet turned over, or that don't stratify.

Coldwater Period (Fall)
Water Temperature: Low 50°F Range to Freezing
General Fish Mood: Neutral

In lakes and reservoirs that freeze in winter, the Coldwater Period extends from the end of the Turnover Period to ice-up. Although their metabolism slows in response to cooling waters, pike remain active. Early in the Coldwater Period, pike may chase crankbaits, but by the end of the period, slow presentations with livebait work best.

As hours of daylight shorten, weedgrowth, insect hatches, and plankton blooms decline. In lakes where small and intermediate-size pike inhabit weedy flats during summer, they may move deeper and concentrate on steep drop-offs or shift to deeper flats that retain weedgrowth. These areas usually are near the deepest areas

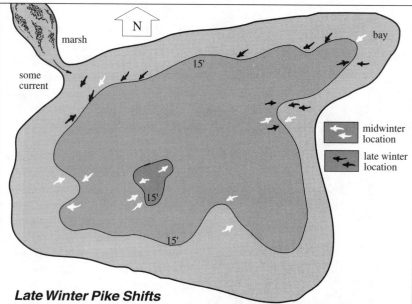

Late Winter Pike Shifts

During most of winter, pike occupy major structural elements that host preyfish and offer substantial living space. Points, bars, islands, and large mid-depth flats provide these needs. Pike congregate in key areas.

In this example, water flowing from the marsh at the north end creates open water off the channel mouth. This cue, in combination with lengthening daylight and internal physiological changes, concentrates fish near the entrance to the marsh—a major spawning site. Pike also congregate near shallow bays suitable for spawning. During late winter, they congregate on obvious structural elements like bars and along weededges adjacent to bays.

of the lake. In reservoirs, pike may gather around points. Drop-offs with forage hold the key to fish location.

The general exodus from the shallows in the early stages of the Coldwater Period often produces concentrations of big fish. Feeding intensity, however, can vary from intense to lockjaw, depending on many environmental factors.

The Coldwater Period is a time of stability. Though pike may bite well, they do so at a slower pace than in spring or fall. The combination of stability and cool water make pike a top target during this period.

Winter or Frozen Water Period

Water Temperature: Annual Minimum For an Extended Time
General Fish Mood: Neutral

On southern reservoirs with pike, ice cover is rare or nonexistent. There, the Winter Period is a continuation of the Fall Coldwater Period that lasts as long as water is near its annual minimum temperature for an extended time.

Bodies of water that contain reproducing populations of pike are ice covered for at least several weeks. In the northern fringe of the pike's natural range, frozen water can last six months or more, bringing stable though challenging environmental conditions.

Ecosystems in lakes move slowly, but pike seem to feed regularly. Growth studies reveal pike adding inches and pounds during this period. Many of the largest pike of the year fall to ice anglers or spear fishermen.

Pike of all sizes are free to roam during the Frozen Water Period. They tend to relate, however, to prey of the appropriate size. They eat deadbait that drifts to the bottom or gets caught in the bottom layers of the ice. Pike are opportunistic feeders, which makes them scavengers during cold months of the year. This behavior remains predictable even as spawning movements begin in late winter or early spring.

**First-ice and last-ice
are prime time for huge pike.**

YEAR OF THE WALLEYE

Secrets to Seasonal Periods of Response

Stocking and dispersal have put walleyes in the home waters of millions of anglers who live outside the native range of this species. Its challenging habits and its highly valued palatability have bolstered walleye popularity wherever it's found. But in its native range, areas like Minnesota and the Dakotas, fishing for most anglers equals walleye fishing. Why pursue other species?

This great popularity is maintained despite sometimes low catch rates. During summer, an angler with a couple fish often should feel successful. Creel surveys demonstrate high catch rates during certain periods on prime walleye waters but low catch rates on many smaller lakes and reservoirs. This need not be so since walleyes are aggressive predators that readily bite lures and livebait.

The key is to fish where walleyes are feeding when they're most active. The In-Fisherman Calendar Periods help anglers define these times in order to crack the biological code of the walleye.

Coldwater Period (Spring)

Water Temperature: Warming Slightly from Annual Minimum
General Fish Mood: Neutral

In northern parts of the walleye range, prespawn movements may begin at the end of the Frozen Water Period, rendering the Spring Coldwater Period hardly distinguishable. A Coldwater Period may occur in years with early ice-out, however. And in more southern walleye waters, the spring Coldwater Period begins with the first rise in the thermometer, accompanied by lengthening days.

This period is one of staging before movements to spawning areas begin or after reaching staging areas. Walleyes move from deep offshore humps to shallower structure, particularly along shorelines with points, rockpiles, and other features that provide cover and attract prey. In reservoirs, walleyes gather in holes at the mouths of tributaries or in deep channel areas in the lower portions of creeks that provide spawning habitat. As the sun warms shallow bays, walleyes also wander in to feed on preyfish that have entered the area to feed on plankton or bottom-dwelling invertebrates

Groups of shallow, deep, or staging walleyes provide good fishing once they're located on sonar or by fishing likely areas. Fish on deeper structure seem to bite better and can be fished for slowly with vertical presentations. Walleyes in shallow bays often are taken incidentally by crappie anglers.

Prespawn Period
Water Temperature: *Upper 30°F to low 40°F Range*
General Fish Mood: *Neutral*

The Prespawn Period begins as walleyes move from wintering areas toward spawning locations. Such journeys may be short as in small lakes or rivers, or extensive as in large lakes, large reservoirs, and the Great Lakes. In expansive systems, individuals may swim over 100 miles to reach spawning areas. They often bypass apparently appropriate spawning sites, returning to more distant areas where they spawned previously. Some biologists suspect that walleyes return to the area where they hatched, in the manner of salmon, but this hasn't been fully documented.

As prespawn walleyes approach the Spawn Period, after dark they move shallow on rock-rubble bars or into rubble-bottomed feeder creeks.

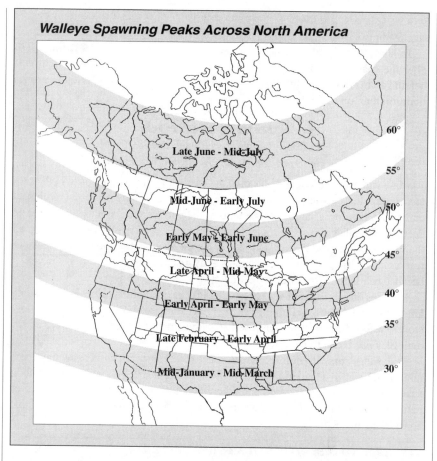

Walleye Spawning Peaks Across North America

In northern waters, the migration begins shortly before or just after ice-out, late winter in southern waters. Males lead the progression to spawning grounds, which may be shallow rocky areas in a lake or reservoir, or shoals in a tributary river. When water temperatures are in the 40°F range, a powerful light can easily spot males on spawning grounds at night. Biologists use this method to count a spawning population.

Where spawning migrations are blocked by dams, walleyes concentrate there prior to spawning. In reservoirs, where riprap banks simulate natural spawning areas better then any other features, walleyes congregate along them. Offshore humps or rocky deltas at the mouths of feeder creeks also draw fish.

Walleyes feed regularly throughout winter, and warming waters spur continued feeding as well as migration. Consider, however, that anglers must adjust their pace from the highly successful but nearly static approach of ice fishing to fishing open water from a boat.

Slow-moving presentations in key areas spell success, and bank anglers often score if migrating or spawning fish are within range. Walleyes hit crankbaits, spoons, spinners, and livebait. Concentrated fish compensate for less than aggressive feeding.

In some states and provinces, closed seasons prohibit walleye fishing until after the spawn, because in some cases, huge aggregations of fish become vulnerable to overharvest. In other situations, the season opener is based more on tradition than on biology.

Spawn Period
Water Temperature: *43°F to 52°F*
General Fish Mood: *Neutral to Negative*

Male walleyes precede females onto the spawning grounds, but once both sexes are present, they waste little time. Most spawning activity is nocturnal, with several males chasing a larger female across a shoal. Some females may stage in deeper holes adjacent to spawning areas while their eggs ripen. But they drop all their eggs within a day or two and then begin the journey back to the main lake or reservoir. In rivers, major movements may not occur as soon after spawning because nearby features offer cover and prey.

Females broadcast from 40,000 to 600,000 eggs, with larger females producing larger clutches. Eggs stick to the rough surfaces of gravel or lodge between larger stones, where current or moderate wave action keep them aerated and free of silt until they hatch one to three weeks later.

Males may run with milt for several weeks and most remain in spawning areas until females have departed; then they follow the females. Males can be caught on spawning areas since they feed sporadically and also aggressively strike lures or baits. Females staging in spawning areas also can be caught, though action is slow considering the abundance of fish.

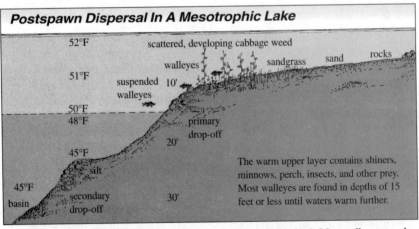

Postspawn Dispersal In A Mesotrophic Lake

52°F — scattered, developing cabbage weed — sandgrass — sand — rocks
walleyes
51°F — suspended walleyes 10'
50°F
48°F — primary drop-off
20'
45°F — silt
45°F basin — secondary drop-off — 30'

The warm upper layer contains shiners, minnows, perch, insects, and other prey. Most walleyes are found in depths of 15 feet or less until waters warm further.

The upper warmer layer of a lake contains most of the available food. Most walleyes remain in this zone, either hiding in shallow weeds, logs, or boulders, or suspending in the shade of a steep drop-off.

Consistent fishing means putting percentages in your favor. In this case, concentrate on the bulk of the walleyes, which generally remain fairly shallow at this time of year.

Postspawn Period

Water Temperature: Low 50°F Range
General Fish Mood: Neutral to Negative

Female and then most male walleyes evacuate spawning shoals once the ripe eggs have been fertilized. Walleyes provide no parental care, so feeding quickly resumes. Postspawn walleyes are notoriously hard to catch, but part of the problem lies in finding groups of fish, not in their reluctance to bite.

In some lakes and rivers, walleyes move gradually deeper after spawning. Finding fish can be simple once you determine where they spawn. Find nearby feeding flats with adjacent deep water and you'll find walleyes. Typical feeding depth for postspawn walleyes ranges from 6 to 20 feet, depending on water clarity, structural features, and dominant preyfish. Uniformly cool water and high oxygen content offer walleyes and other species the freedom to choose holding areas that provide the most prey.

Where shiners, perch, or other panfish provide forage, walleyes hold shallow, particularly at night. Where shad, alewives, or ciscoes are important prey, they suspend off structure or near schools of baitfish.

Night fishing often provides the best bite shortly after the spawn, but feeding peaks at dusk and dawn soon becomes typical. Postspawn walleyes in rivers are easy to find, since they hold near current breaks.

In systems where walleyes make major migrations, locating postspawn fish is tougher since they may move many miles in one day. Check with regional fishery biologists who often have conducted tagging or biotelemetry studies to document walleye movements. Such reports provide valuable information even if they're not recent, since movement patterns often are specific to the population and vary little from year to year.

Presummer Period

Water Temperature: Mid-50°F Range to Low 60°F Range
General Fish Mood: Neutral to Positive

The Presummer Period continues the trend toward summer fishing patterns that began at the end of the Postspawn Period. Yet because various patterns are developing and groups of fish are moving, fishing success can be sporadic. A hot bite one evening may be followed by only a few stragglers the next day.

The key to success during the Presummer Period is in checking many areas and depths with a variety of lures and bait. Select shiners, fathead minnows, chubs, leeches, crawlers, and any other locally popular bait, giving them sufficient soak time to determine what walleyes want.

Trolling, rigging, jigging, or float fishing on shoreline structures, offshore bars, or in open water may work best on an individual outing. Monitor sonar closely for suspended fish and also for how fish are relating to structure. One problem is that other species may be in the same spots as walleyes, so don't waste too much time on fish that refuse to bite. Keep moving.

Weed Walleyes

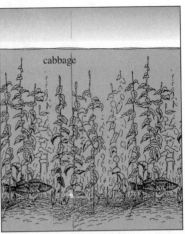

Productive weed types for walleyes include heavy coontail umbrellas where fishing is tough because fish swim underneath and are difficult to reach. Pondweeds (cabbage) often are sparse enough to fish through. Walleyes hold along edges or among stalks.

Summer Peak Period

Water Temperature: Mid-60°F Range to Low 70°F Range
General Fish Mood: Positive

The Summer Peak is a short period, lasting perhaps one to two weeks, during which a lake or reservoir suddenly blooms with life. Spawning is over for most fish, and tiny fry teem in the shallows and over open water. Predators probably can't tell them apart any better than we can and probably don't care.

Young perch, shad, shiners, crappie, bluegills, carp, and other species are prey. Active walleyes may roam from two feet of water (usually at night) down to 30 feet or more until thermal stratification develops to restrict them to above the thermocline.

The Summer Peak is most obvious in lakes and reservoirs, but an analogous situation occurs in rivers, where high production of young fish and increased metabolisms due to quickly warming waters spur fast fishing. Blooming aquatic plants that typify this period in lakes may not be present in rivers, and increased production of plankton also isn't pronounced.

Fishing on all types of waters typically is good though high fishing pressure increases competition for key spots and gradually increases the spookiness of walleyes. Time to explore new patterns or styles of fishing, or to look for "secret" lakes.

Summer Period

Water Temperature: Annual Maximum for an Extended Period
General Fish Mood: Variable—Negative to Positive

The Summer Period may begin in late spring in southern waters and not until late July in the far north. In the South, it's the longest period, second only to the

Winter Period in the North.

Walleyes have established feeding patterns that remain stable for weeks or even longer. Their degree of activity, however, varies according to weather patterns and preyfish behavior. During summer, a cloudy, windy day with a dropping barometer is the time to go fishing. Such conditions often produce the hottest bite of the year.

On clear, cool, and breezy days, go to work. On sunny, hot, calm days, take the kids water skiing. Walleyes can be found, but they rarely bite well. Dawn, dusk, and several hours after dark offer the best fishing. Darker waters typically produce a better daytime bite.

River fishing often is good, as current and murkier water seem to keep walleyes more willing to bite predictably. Holding areas also are more easily defined in all weather conditions.

Postsummer

Water Temperature: *Cooling Substantially from Annual Peak*
General Fish Mood: *Neutral to Positive*

The Postsummer Period is a reversal of the warming Presummer Period. Warm days yield to ever cooler nights as daylight shortens and the intensity of the sun's rays lessens in the northern hemisphere. This period is a winding down of the summer feeding time for warmwater and coolwater fish, but fishing patterns may remain rather intact until this period ends with the Fall Turnover Period.

Walleyes tend to occupy more vertical structure than during the Summer Period. Steep shoreline breaks and pinnacle-like humps hold an increasing number of walleyes, though their precise location and typical holding depth must be determined by fishing. And walleye location may change from day to day or during a day or night.

Walleyes that have spent the summer on flats in thick beds of aquatic vegetation may shift to rock structure or to beds of coontail, bladderwort, and other hardier plants as species like cabbage (broadleaf pondweed) turn brown. Again, fish shift to spots with easy access to deep water.

Walleye in most, but not all environments spend most of their time hunting for food near bottom.

Once you find walleyes, however, they may bite readily even during daylight. Windy days spur the bite in shallow cover, while fish holding deeper may bite in bright sun at mid-day. Still, true to their basic nature, most walleye feeding continues to peak during twilight periods.

Turnover Period

Water Temperature: Upper 50°F Range to Low 50°F Range
General Fish Mood: Neutral to Negative

Turnover is the most dramatic change that occurs in a lake or reservoir. The three layers of water that for several months have been characterized by different temperatures, oxygen concentrations, and other water quality parameters suddenly mix.

In some situations, the thermocline may slowly erode as the warm surface layer of water cools and wind pushes it down to the upper part of the thermocline. But turnover is dramatic in some lakes where water color changes as particles of debris dislodged from the bottom float to the surface or suspend in midwater. In eutrophic systems, hydrogen sulfide gas arising from the depths may give the lake a sulfurous odor for a day or two.

As walleyes and other fish are affected by turnover, fishing invariably slows. Fish may be upset by sudden changes in their environment, as aquarium fish are when a new filter is added or the water changed. More likely, though, fish quickly shift locations in response to changing temperature, oxygen, and water color.

Periods of warm stable weather often produce good fishing during fall.

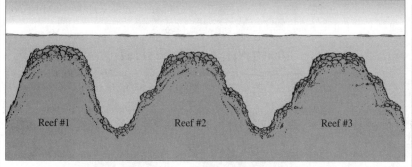

Reef #1   Reef #2   Reef #3

While *Reef #1* will attract walleyes, its ability to hold them during the off-hours is limited because of its steep drop-off. That's why it can hold only a limited number of fish, even though the top may be quite large.

Reef #3 in contrast has a series of stair-steps, which provide a more suitable off-hours environment. Walleyes have more room, which translates into more fish.

Reef #2 is better than *Reef #1* because it has a stair-step and more off-hours room. *Reef #3* is best because it has more adjacent lateral area and more levels of stair-steps.

Walleyes may eat less as they adjust. For whatever reason, turnover slows fishing, so relocate to a river, a lake still the in Postsummer Period, or to one advanced into the Fall Coldwater Period.

Coldwater Period (Fall)

Water Temperature: Low 50°F Range to Annual Minimum
General Fish Mood: Neutral to Positive

Effects of turnover soon vanish as waters clear and all areas hold sufficient oxygen for fish. Location shifts noticeable in the Postsummer Period are intensified. Walleyes favor fast-breaking structure, but their choice of depth remains varied.

Trolling shallow-running minnow baits after dark seems to work almost everywhere. Yet jigging or livebait rigging along 40-foot-deep structural features can take big fish all day. As ice-up approaches, however, slower presentations become dominant.

Vertical jigging with leadheads or spoons, in the ice-fishing manner, can be deadly in lakes, reservoirs, and rivers. Livebait goes from optional at the start of the Coldwater Period to nearly essential at its close. Few anglers take advantage of this period.

Winter or Frozen Water Period

Water Temperature: Annual Minimum for an Extended Period
General Fish Mood: Variable—Negative to Positive

Lakes and reservoirs freeze throughout most of the walleye range but remain open in much of the lower third of the United States. Where waters don't freeze,

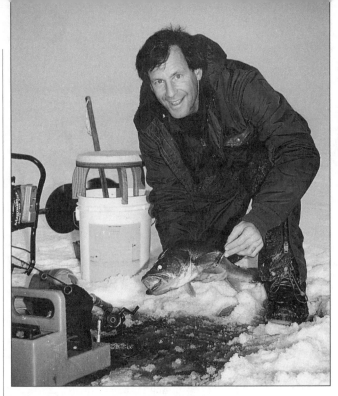

There's no finer time than first-ice to bag a big walleye. Recent advances in ice tackle and paraphernalia make ice fishing a pleasant affair.

the Coldwater Period extends through winter, since patterns remain similar.

Fishing through the ice presents its own challenges, but often the way walleyes relate to structure and respond to baits is similar from the end of the Coldwater Period into the Frozen Water Period. Fishing at early-ice often is excellent on offshore humps or along turns and points on steep structure along prominent mainlake bars.

Walleyes in deep lakes and reservoirs seem to favor humps and structural features of shoreline breaks in the 20- to 40-foot range. Groups of fish hold near these spots for weeks at a time, so fish them regularly and thoroughly. Walleyes typically feed within a foot of the bottom, so keep baits down unless sonar shows fish hovering higher.

Prime fishing occurs at dawn, dusk, and within a couple hours after dark. Action may be sporadic throughout the day and night.

Rivers that remain ice-free can provide excellent winter fishing for walleyes concentrated in areas with reduced current. Anchor and drift baits through these spots or maneuver through high-percentage areas and vertically jig with leadheads or spoons tipped with minnows.

YEAR OF THE SMALLMOUTH BASS

Secrets to Seasonal Periods of Response

Smallmouth bass, arguably North America's toughest freshwater fish, is pursued by anglers wherever it's abundant. Smallmouths inhabit clear natural lakes throughout the lower latitudes of Canada and the northern third of the United States, including the Great Lakes. Smallmouths also thrive in rivers ranging from small Ozark creeks to the mighty Mississippi River. Impoundments in the mid-South provide such good habitat for brown bass that they reach their maximum size in these milder climates.

Wherever they live, smallmouths are mobile, puzzling to even expert anglers with their major vertical and horizontal movements. The In-Fisherman Calendar Periods provide a basis to predict these shifts, giving you a chance to predict movements and migrations so you can consistently catch these mighty sportfish.

Coldwater Period (Spring)

Water Temperature: *Upper 30°F to Mid-40°F*
General Fish Mood: *Neutral to Positive*

The spring Coldwater Period is a time of preparation—a prelude to the annual spawning ritual. This period can be subdivided into an early period and a late period. Smallmouth location and attitude differ in each.

Year of the Smallmouth Bass

1. Prespawn	4. Presummer	7. Postsummer	10. Winter*
2. Spawn	5. Summer Peak	8. Fall Turnover	
3. Postspawn	6. Summer	9. Coldwater	

*Coldest water of the year.

Gregorian Calendar	Jan	Feb	Mar	Apr	May	June	July	Aug	Sept	Oct	Nov	Dec
Northern Range: U.S. - Canadian Border		10			9	1	2 3 4 5	6	7 8	9		10
Southern Range: TVA Reservoirs	10	9	1	2	3 4 5		6		7	8	9	10

In natural lakes, the early part of the Coldwater Period is characterized by water temperatures ranging from the upper 30°F range to the mid-40s. Initially, smallmouth bass are located in sharp-breaking deep-water wintering areas, relating to the base of various structures, particularly along the transition from harder to softer bottom.

In a typical highland reservoir, smallmouths usually hold near deep-lying wintering areas in channels. These spots often are close to spawning and summer habitat. Most fish movement is unpredictable, of short duration, and usually is near a sharp drop-off or along a river channel. Fish and crayfish serve as the main forage at this time. To catch these smallies, slowly work jigs, spoons, tail spinners, and livebait.

The later portion of the Coldwater Period begins as water temperatures rise toward the mid-40°F range. Smallmouths move closer to the shallows, although not necessarily shallower. They're still usually in 20 to 40 feet of water, but are more aggressive than during the first part of this period.

During periods of warming weather, they're often aggressive and actively feeding. A livebait rig or jig remain good choices. Since smallmouths remain concentrated, expect lots of action by casting into a holding area.

In highland reservoirs, smallmouths begin moving toward spawning sites in bays and coves. Along the way, they use points, bars, and humps, usually composed of rock, gravel, rubble, or clay. Wood—fallen timber or logs—also attracts fish. Many times, smallmouths concentrate at various depths on the inside turn of the upstream area of a sharper-breaking portion of a bar. Under ideal conditions, they make short vertical movements from deep water into the shallows.

Some fish move to the mouths of shoreline coves where the warmer water in a feeder creek accelerates the prespawn process. Usually, though, larger creek arms provide better habitat. Small crankbaits, jigs, spinnerbaits, and livebait are effective presentations.

As prespawn approaches, smallmouths move from deeper water into a shallower prespawn staging area. Still, some fish hold in deeper water near spawning areas like bays, coves, and bars.

Prespawn Period

Water Temperature:
about 46°F to 60°F
General Fish Mood:
Neutral to Positive

Prespawn can be subdivided into three separate phases: early prespawn—about 46°F to 50°F; mid-prespawn—about 50°F to 55°F; and late prespawn—about 55°F to 62°F. Each phase is temperature dependent, and smallmouth location and behavior differs in each. Temperature designations, however, aren't strict since annual variations occur among bodies of water.

Early prespawn is a transition stage. Smallmouths begin vacating deeper staging areas, filtering onto shallow flats. Warm stable weather prompts fish to move. They begin cruising shallow water, seeking potential spawning sites as they search for prey. Smallmouths feed actively, often on crayfish in the shallows, especially during warming trends.

As water temperature nudges into the low 50°F range, smallmouths are in mid-prespawn movement. Most are in shallow water in areas protected from harsh winds and preferably over sand, gravel, broken rock, or rubble bottoms. Rocks, reeds, docks, fallen trees, or other cover draw fish.

At times, smallmouth occupy areas that seem less than optimal. The back portion of a shallow bay, for example, may be used for spawning. There, the water warms rapidly, yet the bottom content isn't choice.

Smallmouths in reservoirs also move closer to spawning areas—backs of coves or onto flat sections of a protruding bar or point in a creek arm. They often select small shoreline pockets with a gravel or rock-rubble bottom.

Spawning Times

Male smallmouth guarding the nest.

Boulders create a strong defensive position.

Guarding newly hatched fry from hungry intruders.

Spawn Period

Water Temperature: 60°F to 67°F
General Fish Mood: Negative

This brief period usually lasts little more than a week for females and several weeks for males. Bass may begin spawning at temperatures as low as 55°F and as high as the 70°F range. Environmental factors such as weather, angle of the sun, and water level also play a role in determining when bass spawn.

Male smallmouths build nests at a depth dependent on water clarity, from 18 inches in dingy water to 20 feet in ultraclear water. Most nests, however, are in 2 to 5 feet of water, near cover with a gravel or rubble bottom. Most nests are at the same depth.

Meanwhile, females are noticeably absent from the extreme shallows, typically holding near small rocky fingers or other deeper-lying cover as they wait for their eggs to ripen. When they're ready to spawn, they enter the shallows.

Bass feed little during spawning. Cantankerous males, however, strike at baits, lures, or other intruders into the nest area as they fan the nest to provide oxygen, remove wastes, and prevent siltation. Eggs hatch in 2 to 10 days, depending on water temperature. The male remains on guard until the fry disperse from the nest. In northern parts of the smallmouth range, regulations often prohibit fishing for smallmouth during the Spawn Period.

Postspawn Period

Water Temperature: 65°F and Above
General Fish Mood: Negative to Neutral

The behavior of male and female bass differs during this period. After spawning, males aggressively guard nests against predation. Females, meanwhile, are

Rigged and Ready for Shallow Water
(less than 10 feet deep)

Tackle	Lakes	Rivers	Reservoirs
6' medium spinning, 6- or 8-lb. test	1/8-oz. jig (Mister Twister Meeny, Lindy-Little Joe Fuzz-E-Grub, Blue Fox Foxee)	1/8-oz. jig (Northland Fire-Ball, Berkley Power Grub, Mann's Swimmin' Grub)	1/8-oz. jig (generic tube, Bait Rigs Slo-Poke, Mann's Sting Ray Grub)
6½' medium-heavy spinning, 8- or 10-lb. test	topwater or minnow imitator (Rapala, Heddon Tiny Torpedo, Bagley Balsa B)	#2 straight-shaft spinner (Mepps, Panther Martin, Blue Fox Vibrax)	topwater or slow sinker (Rebel Pop-R, Heddon Zara Puppy, Lunker City Slug-Go)
6' medium casting, 10- or 12-lb. test	shallow-diving crankbait (Rebel Wee-R, Cordell Big O, Norman Little N)	shallow diving crankbait (Storm Wiggle Wart, Bagley DB-2, Bomber Model A)	clear water, sparse cover— previously mentioned topwaters and crankbaits
6' medium-heavy casting, 12- or 14-lb. test	deep-diving crankbait (Rapala Shad Rap, Poe's RC 1, Rebel Deep Wee-R)	sinking crankbait (Bill Lewis Rat-L-Trap, Cordell Spot, Mann's Manniac)	dark water or wood cover— 1/4- or 3/8-oz. spinnerbaits (Berkley Power Spin, Bass Pro Shops, Stanley Vibra-Shaft)

While more anglers fish for largemouths, some surveys indicate that most anglers prefer to catch smallmouths.

unaggressive, probably still holding near spawning areas but in deeper water. Thus begins the postspawn dispersal.

Smallmouths in lakes, rivers, and reservoirs have different options available to them and thus react differently. Smallmouths in reservoirs vacate the immediate spawning area, relocating adjacent to it. Some move to deeper water at the mouths of coves. Others drop into deeper water near spawning bars. Still others seek shallow rocky areas with wood cover. If forage is available on or near a spawning area, however, some smallmouths remain nearby, perhaps for most of the season.

Presummer Period

Water Temperature: Upper 60°F to 70°F Range
General Fish Mood: Neutral to Positive

A resumption of feeding activities indicates the beginning of the Presummer Period, though no absolute temperature indicates when fish enter this period. Surface temperatures typically have warmed over 70°F and smallmouths need lots of food.

This is a time of emerging weedgrowth and developing food chains. Depending on the body of water, prey might include shad, alewives, smelt, crayfish, sculpin, shiners, larval and adult insects, and frogs. Presummer is characterized by a variety of successful fishing patterns—livebait rigs in deep water, crankbaits on mid-depth flats, or surface baits near shoreline cover.

Summer Peak Period

Water Temperature: 70°F to 75°F
General Fish Mood: Positive

The Summer Peak Period is a short period of fine fishing. A span of warm, often calm weather triggers fish to move from the Presummer Period into the Summer Peak. This often is the season's first spell of hot weather.

Most organisms in a body of water are blooming. Insect hatches are thick.

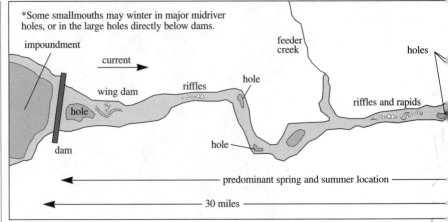

*Some smallmouths may winter in major midriver holes, or in the large holes directly below dams.

impoundment

current

wing dam

riffles

hole

feeder creek

holes

riffles and rapids

hole

dam

hole

predominant spring and summer location

30 miles

The map depicts a 30-mile river section between dams. Most of the flowing river section is less than 10 feet deep, with a few deeper holes. A variety of riffles, holes, and runs with rock, rock-rubble, and sand substrate plus cool water provide excellent smallmouth habitat.

In fall, bass leave areas of strong current, moving either to deep holes or to a downstream impoundment. The wide body of the reservoir dissipates current, and fish act much as they would in a lake. Deep points and humps become prime attractors. In shallow reservoirs, the river channel provides key deep-water access. In deeper impoundments, bass usually have more options.

Feeder creeks are an overlooked option in early to mid-fall if rain raises the water level enough to allow smallmouths access to them.

Rooted weedgrowth is maturing, and weedlines are becoming obvious. Fish seek prey in a variety of habitats.

A combination of environmental factors stimulates Summer Peak activity. First, fish are hungry, aggressive, and catchable. Larger female bass begin grouping, and this competitive group activity stimulates feeding. Look for optimal structures—ponds, humps, and saddles—and fish the best cover in these areas.

Summer Period
Water Temperature: *Maximum for a Body of Water*
General Fish Mood: *Neutral to Positive*

The Romans believed the dog star Sirius rose with the sun, giving the days of July and August a double measure of heat. Thus the term "dog days," which implies lethargy among fish. That, though, is an illusion. During the Summer Period, bass are in high gear. Abundant prey are available in the form of fry and fingerling fish, insects, and crayfish. So while bass become selective in their choice of forage, they continue to feed heavily.

Fishing during summer is a challenge because bass scatter over large areas and at various depths. Additionally, feeding times often are short. Low light conditions trigger smallmouths to feed, with nocturnal feeding common in clear lakes, rivers, and reservoirs.

On Canadian Shield lakes, large sunken islands and lip areas composed of

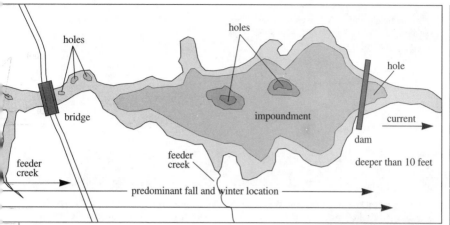

holes

holes

hole

bridge

impoundment

current

dam

feeder creek

feeder creek

deeper than 10 feet

predominant fall and winter location

broken rock, gravel, and rubble become prime smallmouth areas. The presence of weeds makes these prime spots. On many northern natural lakes, smallmouths hold on rock-capped sunken islands and rock-gravel bars. Slow-tapering flats with sandgrass on the deeper edges also attract bass.

In reservoirs, smallmouths also scatter. Some almost always hold on long points or rounded bluff points on the main reservoir. A few move to steep, rocky banks with isolated fallen trees. Deeper humps or submerged islands also attract bass. These areas provide cover, along with forage such as crayfish, young-of-the-year fish, and shad.

In clear highland reservoirs where some smallmouths suspend near bluff points in deeper water during the day, they move to feed in shallower areas with rocks and wood cover at night. During late summer, they may also bust shad on the surface near bluff points.

During stable water flow, bass in rivers often spread over rocky flats to hunt for crawfish. Large rocks on

Smallmouths are noted leapers. They're one of the gamest freshwater fish of all.

43

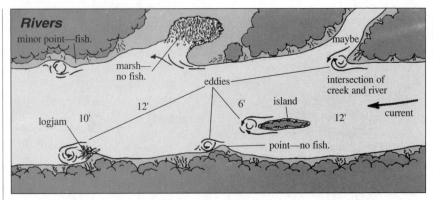

Rivers

minor point—fish.

marsh—
no fish.

maybe

eddies

intersection of
creek and river

12'

6'

island

logjam   10'

12'

current

point—no fish.

High water levels in spring usually push river smallmouths tight to shore behind current-deflecting points, logjams, and islands. Smallies concentrate in eddies that contain the proper combination of depth, bottom content, and cover to ensure spawning success.

Many of the best areas are subtle—downstream tips of islands, small eddies behind minor points, and areas behind logjams. These areas often look the same as dozens of others, but for some reason they tend to concentrate bass. The only way to know for sure is to fish them systematically as you run the river. Concentrate on the shallower inside edges of the calm water where nest construction will likely occur.

Slack-water bays at first appear attractive but seldom are good smallmouth spots. Most smallies associate with the main current flow. They may move up a feeder creek to build nests if adequate conditions exist, but they more likely use the upstream junction where a pocket of calm water forms between two current flows.

such flats concentrate fish. Rattlebaits help find fish fast. During high water, by contrast, bass are pushed into or downcurrent from shoreline cover that diverts current.

Postsummer Period

Water Temperature: Cooling From Annual Maximum
General Fish Mood: Neutral to Positive

Postsummer reverses the Presummer process, a time when a body of water begins to cool. This occurs at the end of summer when warm days are followed by cool nights. Days are growing shorter, a cosmic signal that things are slowing down. Summer's time of plenty is giving way to reduced food stocks.

Early in this period, smallmouths remain scattered in their summer habitat. In lakes and reservoirs, as water temperatures decline, they begin to group along cover edges near deeper water. In rivers, where they're more affected by water level than by water temperature, summer patterns continue.

Turnover Period

Water Temperature: Upper to Low 50°F Range
General Fish Mood: Generally Negative

Waters that don't stratify into three temperature layers during summer don't turn over. Rivers, for example, don't stratify. Shallow wind-tossed bodies of water or those with heavy current usually don't stratify. Yet while the fish in these waters aren't affected by a Turnover Period, the fish still must adjust to a progressively colder environment.

Most lakes and reservoirs remain stratified throughout the Summer Peak, Summer, and Postsummer periods. Then, cold winds, rain, and chilly nights cool the surface temperature. As the heavier colder water sinks, it mixes with warmer water below, creating currents that gradually wear away the narrow thermocline layer. As the thermocline breaks down, mixing or "turning over" continues reoxygenating the depths.

Fishing often is difficult during the Turnover Period. All bodies of water don't, however, turn over at the same time. Switch to a lake that hasn't turned over, or to waters that don't stratify, or to one that has already turned over and is again stable.

If you fish a lake under Turnover conditions, seek the best available shallow cover near deep water. Areas of shallow broken rock with weeds or wood are good choices.

Call him bronzeback, brown bass, or mean machine, the small-mouth is active throughout the Coldwater Period and into winter.

Coldwater Period (Fall)
Water Temperature: *Low 50°F Range to Annual Minimum*
General Fish Mood: *Neutral to Positive*

During the Coldwater Period, water temperature continues to slowly decline, and smallmouth metabolism slows in response. Smallmouths also begin shifting into deeper-lying areas. Most vacate shallow flats for areas along the base of drop-offs near summer habitat. During stable, warm, sunny weather, groups of small-mouths may still move shallow and scatter to prominent shallow cover on flats. After feeding, however, they return to deeper water.

Many prime drop-off areas in lakes are far from shore and near a mid-depth portion of the lake basin. In highland reservoirs, smallmouths congregate near steeper-dropping points and bluffs in the main reservoir or in portions of creek arms with deep water. Prime areas have cover—boulders, rock, rubble, and stumps, along with steep drop-offs.

This is a great time to catch big bass. They're concentrated, catchable, and as heavy as they'll be until late Prespawn. For chances for a trophy, generally try 12- to 40-foot depths with a jig'n pig, jig and grub, or a tailspinner.

Winter or Frozen Water Period
Water Temperature: Coldest for an Extended Period
General Fish Mood: Inactive

The Winter Period is the longest period of the coldest water of the year. Ice cover is common in the north. In southern reservoirs, ice cover may occur briefly in coves and wind-protected bays. Rivers may or may not ice over, depending on current and geographical location.

Smallmouth bass may be somewhat active at first-ice, but eventually in most lakes and reservoirs that ice over, they become lethargic as they group in deep-water sanctuaries.

About a month before ice-out bass begin to stir. Find a concentration of fish, and you can catch a few on ice lures baited with waxworms or a minnow head.

In rivers, bass often retreat to deeper holes and may be catchable on jigs or live-bait. Higher water moves them into shoreline pockets that provide protection against heavy current flow. They're catchable on jigs and livebait.

The best fishing in reservoirs during this period occurs during spells of warm stable weather. Look for fish at the mouths of feeder creeks or off points on the interior of large deep feeder creeks. Try jigging spoons or grubs. Smallmouths sometimes hold so deep, however, that releasing them alive is difficult, due to expansion of the gas bladder that prevents fish from swimming down. If this occurs, don't fish for deep fish.

Anglers along the East Coast have found river smallmouths catchable throughout mild winters. This probably doesn't apply to rivers in north central North America, but might apply across the South and along the West Coast.

YEAR OF THE LARGEMOUTH BASS

Secrets to Seasonal Periods of Response

I n North America, large-mouth bass range from southern Ontario to central Mexico. While bass behave similarly throughout their range, timing and length of prespawn activities, hibernation, and other behaviors vary. Our 10 Calendar Periods of fish response categorize bass behavior by season. Understanding Calendar Periods is one basis for consistent fishing success on a variety of lakes, rivers, reservoirs, pits, and ponds.

While water temperature is an important impetus for seasonal shifts, it doesn't work like a switch. For example:

• No magic temperature pulls bass into the shallows for a prespawn feeding spree or triggers

them to spawn.

• Bass respond to temperature trends more than to degrees on a thermometer.

• Temperatures in one part of a lake or reservoir can vary substantially from temperatures elsewhere in that body of water. Bass activities in each location vary accordingly.

• Individual bass respond differently to temperature and other environmental factors. Behavior depends on fish size as well as individual differences among fish.

Some Calendar Periods are triggered by events other than temperature. The Presummer Period, for example, is tied to the development of weedy cover, which is dependent on weather.

The Ten In-Fisherman Calendar Periods

1 Prespawn	2 Spawn	3 Postspawn	4 Presummer	5 Summer Peak	6 Summer	7 Postsummer	8 Turnover	9 Coldwater	10 Winter

Coldwater Period (Spring)

Water Temperature: Cold but Rising
General Fish Mood: Inactive to Neutral

This period occurs as early as late January in the South and as late as the end of April in the most northern regions of the largemouth range, as water warms from the low-40°F range into the 50°F range.

Bass move from deep-lying wintering sites toward the shallows where they resume feeding and later spawn. Bass in reservoirs typically move along creek channels or over deep flats. They sometimes hold in large aggregations where cover and baitfish are present. For bass in coldwater reservoirs, 10 to 20 feet is

Periods of warm stable sunny spring weather warms shallow water quickly, attracting minnow forage and bass.

their average depth during early spring. Fish in lakes move shallower more quickly because deep cover is sparse. The spring Coldwater Period is short in northern lakes where water warms rapidly after ice-out.

In the South, where bass shift areas over a longer period of time, fishing can be good, especially for big fish. Observant anglers can find holding areas that bass visit each year for a week or two. Typical locations are timbered holes in submerged creek channels near expansive flats or sloughs. As water warms, bass

Largemouth Bass Calendar

1. Prespawn
2. Spawn
3. Postspawn

4. Presummer
5. Summer Peak
6. Summer

7. Postsummer
8. Fall Turnover
9. Coldwater

10. Winter*

*Coldest water of the year.

Gregorian Calendar	Jan	Feb	Mar	Apr	May	June	July	Aug	Sept	Oct	Nov	Dec
Northern Range	10			9	1	2, 3, 4, 5		6	7	8	9	10
Mid Range	10		9	1	2, 3, 4, 5			6	7	8	9	10
Southern Range	10	9	1	2	3, 4, 5	6			7	8	9	10

The 10 Calendar Periods of fish response can vary in length as much as four weeks from one year to the next. The periods aren't based on the Gregorian calendar, so they don't occur on specific dates each year. Instead, the Calendar periods are based on nature's clock.

In addition, the Calendar Periods vary by regions of the country. Southern waters have an extended Summer Period and a brief Winter Period. In contrast, lakes along the US-Canadian border have extended Coldwater and Winter periods. Bass in Florida or Texas could be in the Spawning Period while those in Minnesota are still in the Winter Period.

scatter toward shallower spawning and feeding sites.

Soon after ice-out, bass in northern lakes move shallow into black-bottom bays or canals. They're spooky but can be caught on slowly worked presentations like tube jigs or unweighted plastic worms.

In many northern states, bass season is closed at this time, and where it's open, fishing can be inconsistent because of changeable weather.

Prespawn Period

Water Temperature: Cool but Rising
General Fish Mood: Positive

As the water warms, bass move shallower. Dark-bottom bays, particularly those on northwest shores, warm first, drawing panfish, minnows, and predator species. Insect activity also is greater here than in the main lake. Bass gather around limited available cover including weed and lily pad stalks, stumps, and fallen trees.

Warming coves and shallow creek arms in reservoirs draw prey species. Clear water that's warmer attracts bass, so dead-end creeks and sloughs provide better fishing than creeks with current. Because bass see better and therefore bite better in clear water, upper reservoir reaches muddied by late-winter rains often don't produce well. Clearer shallow coves in the lower third of the reservoir often yield better catches when water temperatures are in the 50°F range.

Bass movement toward the shallows sometimes is tentative. They move into warming shallow bays, but retreat during wind or cold fronts to the first drop-off with substantial cover. Under adverse conditions, they more likely remain in coves with thick cover.

Most preyfish species move shallow during the Prespawn Period. Bass must feed heavily to complete the maturation of eggs and sperm and to store energy for the Spawn Period. Water levels in natural lakes, reservoirs, and rivers typically are higher than at any other season. Seek active bass in shoreline cover and in flooded brush, trees, and terrestrial plants.

During late prespawn, bass are aggressive and catchable. Cold blustery weather turns fish off early in the Prespawn Period, but as the spawn approaches, they're almost always active, especially in northern waters. Warm, stable weather for several days can produce fantastic fishing. Often the best fishing is toward evening on sunny days.

Switch lakes for the longest possible prespawn fishing. By moving among bodies of water, prespawn fishing can be stretched more than a month in northern waters, two months in the South. Water temperatures must steadily rise into the low 60°F range and remain there before spawning begins. Bass in the South typically remain in the Prespawn Period at higher temperatures than bass in northern regions who spawn at lower temperatures.

Spawn Period

Water Temperature: Moderately Warm and Rising
General Fish Mood: Neutral, But Aggressively Defensive

Several factors trigger the spawn, the most important being length of daylight and water temperature. Water temperature rising into the low 60°F range shifts male bass from prespawn feeding to nest preparation. But bass in a body of water don't all spawn at the same time. Indeed, they've spawned in water temperatures from the high 50s to the low 80s. Water temperature also may vary among sections of a body of water. This scattered spawning protects an entire year class from being destroyed by adverse weather.

In reservoirs, bass usually spawn earliest in the upper reaches, latest in the lower portion, because upstream coves and creek arms usually are shallower

Typical Spawning Months

AREA	MONTHS
Florida	February and March
Mississippi	March through early April
Missouri	April
Pennsylvania	May
Minnesota/Ontario	mid-May to late June

The timing of the largemouth bass Spawn Period illustrates the region-by-region progression of Calendar Periods. Latitude, water temperature, weather trends, length of daylight, competition for habitat, and an internal clock are some of the factors influencing the exact timing of the spawn.

Not all bass spawn at the same time, even in the same body of water. While most adult bass in a lake may spawn during a couple weeks of ideal conditions, some spawn earlier, some later. Regionally, the onset of largemouth bass spawning may begin in February in the South and late June in Ontario.

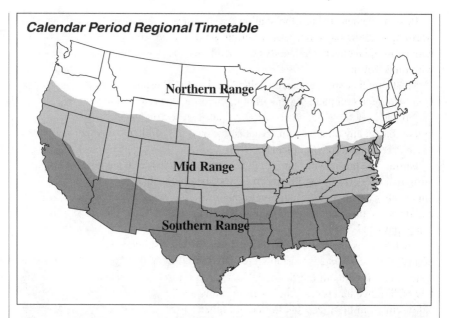

Calendar Period Regional Timetable

Northern Range

Mid Range

Southern Range

and darker colored and thus warm faster in the upper reaches. Spawning may continue for four to six weeks in a reservoir. Larger bass tend to spawn earlier than smaller bass. A spawning area filled with small fish may indicate that the spawn is almost completed.

Largemouth bass have spawned successfully in water from 6 inches to 15 feet deep, but they typically nest in water 1 to 4 feet deep. The murkier the water, the shallower they spawn. Spawning versatility is yet another aspect of bass adaptability.

Because silt can smother and destroy fertilized eggs, and because predators seek eggs for their protein content, male bass must choose nest sites carefully. They often choose sites in channels, coves, bays, and along wind-protected shores. In rivers, bass seek quiet backwaters with medium to hard bottoms.

Males sweep away the fine debris to form a silt-free rounded nest site on a firm bottom. In late-stage eutrophic lakes with softer bottoms, bass may bed on roots of aquatic plants. They often sweep out nests next to a rock, log, or weed stalks to reduce the area they must guard against egg stealers like sunfish, bullheads, perch, and shiners.

After sweeping a nest, a male courts a larger female with nips, bumps, and short chases until they both position over the nest. Spawning commences. A female deposits 2,000 to 7,000 eggs which the male simultaneously fertilizes. Female bass may deposit a second batch of eggs on another nest hours or days later, often fertilized by a different male.

Males defend the nest and fan the eggs to provide oxygen, remove waste products, and prevent siltation. Females remain shallow only until they've expelled their eggs. They will strike various baits at this time. Many trophy bass are caught

Cover keys finding largemouths in most environments during all seasons.

(where fishing is legal) during the spawn.

Males remain on nests to defend them and often strike lures that fall into or hover over the nest. The aggressiveness of their defense depends on weather conditions, fishing pressure, and the stage of egg development.

Males fan and guard their eggs for two to five days until the eggs hatch. Hatchlings, sustained by their yolk sac, remain in the nest for up to a week. As fry emerge, they aggregate in a dark ball, which the male guards until the fry swim off and begin eating zooplankton.

Because of erratic spring weather, the success of a spawn varies. Even under the most favorable circumstances, only a fraction of one percent of fry reach catchable size. Optimal conditions include high and stable water levels and slowly rising temperatures. Slowly declining water levels usually aren't detrimental, but quickly falling water strands eggs and fry or forces fingerlings into open water where predators lurk.

During the spawn, fishing varies from poor to easy. Males are particularly vulnerable while guarding nests. Females also are vulnerable during the time they're in shallow areas where they're sometimes visible and lure presentation is easy.

In many northern states where the spawn is most synchronized and bass are most vulnerable, regulations prohibit fishing for bass during the spawn or severely limit harvest to prevent overharvest.

Postspawn Period

Water Temperature: *Warming through the 70°F range*
General Fish Mood: *Inactive to Neutral*

Postspawn is a short transition period between completion of reproductive activities and the onset of summer patterns. Bass leave shallow bedding areas and move toward areas they'll use all summer, lingering at times in emerging lily pads and submerged weedbeds growing outside spawning areas.

During postspawn, bass scatter and usually don't move as a group, though numbers of fish may hold in particular areas. They're also not aggressive, due apparently to the physical demands of spawning. Fishing typically is difficult.

Until water warms and weeds reach the surface, bass tend to remain near bottom. Surface lures and spinnerbaits aren't as effective as they were when bass were massed in the shallows or when they're feeding more aggressively. In a given body of water, however, individual bass may be in a Prespawn, Spawn, Postspawn, or Presummer period.

Doug Hannon, the "Bass Professor," has offered many trend-setting observations about largemouth bass in the pages of *In-Fisherman* magazine. While many fishermen consider Prespawn the peak period for giant bass, Hannon focuses on the Summer Period for most of his hundreds of bass over 10 pounds. According to Hannon, summer brings stable weather, stable water conditions, and stable fish reaction. Fishermen, therefore, can key on peak daily and monthly periods of lunar influence.

Presummer Period

Water Temperature: *Warm and Rising*
General Fish Mood: *Positive*

As the water warms and weeds develop, bass move to depths with the best available cover and prey. In natural lakes, large flats often provide this habitat. At first, bass cluster among weed clumps on flats. Later, they move deeper as weeds sprout along deeper breaklines. Active bass feed on the outside or inside edges of weedlines or over the weeds.

In reservoirs, bass move toward the mouths of small sloughs and shoreline points, especially those near a deeper channel with stumps or timber. They often begin preying on shad that move over mainlake flats. Bass typically are aggressive, feeding to recover from spawning. They're catchable on a variety of presentations.

Summer Peak Period

Water Temperature: *Warm and Rising*
General Fish Mood: *Positive*

Summer Peak is a short period when bass first occupy their typical summer locations. Lily pads have formed but aren't covered with algae. Most aquatic plants have developed, producing well-defined inside and outside weededges. Oxygen levels are high and the water's clear. Lakes are stratifying or have stratified.

Food is plentiful, as newly hatched baitfish grow. Adult preyfish have spawned and are vulnerable to large predators. Bass feed aggressively unless early summer

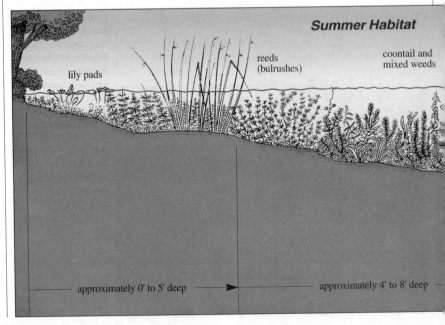

Summer Habitat

lily pads

reeds (bulrushes)

coontail and mixed weeds

approximately 0' to 5' deep ➤

approximately 4' to 8' deep

cold fronts are severe. In reservoirs with strong shad populations, some bass begin to shadow shad schools offshore, particularly at dawn and dusk.

Bass location varies. Some fish are in heavy cover in shallow water while others prowl deep weedlines, timber, and stumpfields. Catch rates typically are high, but large bass are scattered.

During this period, bass may hold in deeper water if forage fish are available. Moderate water temperatures and high oxygen levels allow bass to inhabit various depths. Deeper lying bass are harder to locate but are reliable biters because they aren't so likely to change their activity level with minor weather changes. Aggregations are common on prime structure. Fishing can be terrific.

Summer Period

Water Temperature: *Maximum for a Body of Water*
General Fish Mood: *Variable*

During the Summer Period, water temperatures reach their maximum. Waters that stratify are divided into three zones—a warm surface layer (epilimnion); a layer of rapidly declining temperature (thermocline or metalimnion); and a deep cool layer (hypolimnion) with insufficient oxygen to support bass.

Minnows, shad, sunfish, and other prey are plentiful in the shallow layer. Bass feed heavily, but often briefly, for the abundance of prey reduces competition for food. Fishing may become difficult as bass become finicky and concentrate on specific prey during specific times. In fertile waters, presenting lures or livebait can become difficult because of dense weedgrowth. Low oxygen levels at dawn in fertile waters may hurt fishing during early morning.

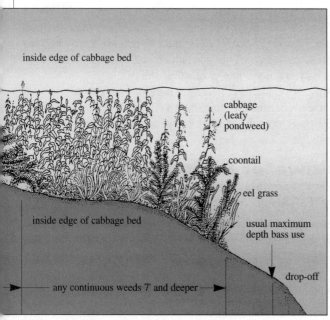

inside edge of cabbage bed

cabbage (leafy pondweed)

coontail

eel grass

inside edge of cabbage bed

usual maximum depth bass use

drop-off

any continuous weeds 7' and deeper

By Summer Peak, bass have settled into areas they use throughout summer. In lakes and many reservoirs, weedbeds become the focus of bass activity. Three general areas include heavy shallow weeds (slop); moderately deep weeds on the flat; and weeds along the deep weededge.

Groups of bass usually hold in many different habitats. Fishing at dusk or at night may provide the best action as large bass leave heavy cover to prowl flats.

Summer is one of the most stable and predictable periods. It's also the longest period in southern climates, up to six months in Florida.

Postsummer Period
Water Temperature: Warm but Cooling
General Fish Mood: Variable

Declining daylight and cooling water gradually alters summer patterns of large-mouth bass behavior. Plants begin to die. Shallow vegetation declines first, then the deep weeds as water becomes murkier due to wind action and plankton blooms. Bass in shallow areas hold near remaining cover, gradually moving to clumps of green weeds remaining in deep water in protected areas such as inside turns.

Bass in reservoirs often move to shallower cover as water temperatures moderate and shad move inshore. Some fish move into small creeks as temperatures decline, but they evacuate these restricted areas when temperatures fall into the low 50°F range. Eventually, dropping water temperatures also reduce the metabolism and feeding requirements of bass.

Postsummer is a transition period. Fishing can be good or poor, depending on how weather conditions affect the variables that give each body of water its own unique characteristics.

Turnover
Water Temperature: Upper to Low 50°F range
General Fish Mood: Inactive

Fall weather cools surface water, making it heavy enough to mix with cooler water in the thermocline. Wind furthers the mixing, as the thermocline narrows and finally disintegrates. As water mixes from surface to bottom, it may become muddy, due to rising bottom debris. Hydrogen sulfide and other gases that were trapped on the bottom may produce a musky or sulfur smell.

Fishing becomes difficult. Conditions leading to turnover may extend over several weeks and contribute to poor fishing throughout a region. On a particular lake, however, turnover rarely lasts more than a week before conditions stabilize and the body of water enters the fall Coldwater Period.

Coldwater Period (Fall)
Water Temperature: Cool, Declining to Cold
General Fish Mood: Moderately Active to Inactive

Following turnover, water usually is in the 50°F range. Cold temperatures and the breakup of summer fishing patterns end the season for many anglers. But this period can yield the biggest bass of the season. Outstanding catches occur when anglers locate groups of bass.

Bass aggregate around remaining cover. In some waters, they move to steeply sloping structure where they can change depths without moving far horizontally.

These areas become winter sanctuaries for large numbers of bass.

Bass that have been buried in shallow weeds all summer move first to cover on flats and finally to cover on or near drop-offs. They're accessible to anglers, often for the first time since spring.

In reservoirs, bass aggregate in creek channels and along outside edges of weedy flats. Where shad school offshore, bass in deep reservoirs remain deep.

While water temperatures remain in the 50°F range, bass may feed aggressively, often chasing lures. Slower presentations tend to maximize the catch in cold water, however, and slower works best for lunker bass.

Green weed patches, usually on drop-offs, key location for bass in natural lakes. Not all weeds die off at the same time. Coontail, for example, thrives in cool water, and lily pads and milfoil hold up late into the season. As fragile species of weeds decline, those that remain attract and concentrate bass.

Fish large baits slowly. When action slows, try smaller, more subtle baits like grubs and thin short worms.

Winter Or Frozen Water Period

Water Temperature: At Its Coldest for an Extended Period
General Fish Mood: Inactive

Winter is a long period that can't be defined by precise environmental conditions since bass are found in a variety of geographical areas. The Winter Period is, however, characterized by the coldest temperatures of the year. In northern Minnesota, water on lakes and even parts of rivers is under three feet of ice. Water temperatures range from about 32°F directly under the ice to 39°F on the bottom. In southern states, water temperatures usually are in the 40°F range, mid-50s in Florida.

Largemouth bass generally hold in the deepest water they use all year. They move deep to water that's slightly warmer and more stable than water near the surface. Just how deep depends on many circumstances; 20 to 30 feet is common in natural lakes, 50 feet in deeper reservoirs. In shallow

Bass bite when the snow flies and when the water freezes, for anglers who know how, where, and when.

The largemouth bass is truly a fish for all seasons. The best ice bites usually occur at first-ice and last-ice, and in ponds and small reservoirs with large populations of bass.

reservoirs or ponds, bass are in or near the deepest available water. Bass in rivers seek backwaters with adequate oxygen and away from current. Preyfish generally also are concentrated on middepth flats in or near the lake basin.

Largemouth bass often gather in huge winter aggregations. In reservoirs, these aggregations often suspend in timber near deep creek channels. Even though bass are inactive, aggregations are so large that a few fish are usually active enough to hit lures.

Cold water reduces bass metabolism. Fish feed infrequently, becoming active only periodically, especially early and late in the Winter Period. Ice fishermen, who usually seek other species, commonly catch largemouth bass through the ice. Lunkers are common just prior to ice-out.

Bass in shallow eutrophic waters are affected by declining oxygen levels in winter as all organisms use oxygen and none is replenished from the air or by photosynthesis. In some lakes, oxygen deprivation in deep water forces bass to move shallower. In shallow lakes in the far north, winterkill may occur.

YEAR OF THE CRAPPIE

Secrets to Seasonal Periods of Response

Crappies follow the rhythm of nature with their own distinct patterns of behavior. As the water warms from spring into summer, black and white crappies respond to the increasing pace of life with more movement and aggressiveness. Then, as the water cools from fall into winter, the tempo of life gradually slows and crappies become more sedentary and selective. Good crappie anglers understand these seasonal tendencies and adjust their tactics to keep in step with nature's changing scene.

These fundamental principles determine crappie location and behavior during each of the In-Fisherman Calendar periods.

Coldwater Period (Spring)
Water Temperature: Upper Range 30°F to about 50°F
General Fish Mood: Neutral

The Spring Coldwater Period is a time of preparation, a prelude to the crappie spawn. It is also a period of transition from the lethargy of winter to the coolwater environment of spring.

In northern lakes, the Spring Coldwater Period begins just after ice-out, with water temperatures in the upper 30°F range. In more southerly waters, it may commence with water temperatures in the low 40°F range, depending on how low the water temperature dropped during the Winter Period. In either case, it arrives as winter grudgingly releases its icy grip and waters begin to warm.

As ice-out occurs in northern natural lakes, crappies typically suspend near major drop-offs. In small lakes and ponds, they may hold in the center of the deepest hole

Crappie Calendar

1. Prespawn
2. Spawn
3. Postspawn
4. Presummer
5. Summer Peak
6. Summer
7. Postsummer
8. Fall Turnover
9. Coldwater
10. Winter*

*Coldest water of the year.

Gregorian Calendar	Jan	Feb	Mar	Apr	May	June	July	Aug	Sept	Oct	Nov	Dec
Northern Range	10	10	10	10	9 / 1	2 3 4 5	6	7 8	9	9	10	10
Mid Range	10	9	1	2	3 4 5	6	6	6	7 8	9	9	10
Southern Range	10	9	1	2	3 4 5	6	6	6	7 8	9	9	

The 10 Calendar Periods of fish response can vary in length from year to year, and in some waters they may overlap. Lengths of periods can vary as much as four weeks from one year to the next.

The Calendar Periods also vary by regions. Crappies in Florida could be in the Spawn Period while those in northern Minnesota are still "iced-up" in the Winter Period.

in the lake, from 5 to 20 feet below the surface. Crappies in reservoirs display a similar tendency, although they tend to be more object-oriented, relating to deep tree-lines and channel edges, rather than suspending away from cover.

Soon after ice-out, stable warm weather, particularly calm sunny days, draws crappies into shallow channels, bays, cuts, harbors, and backwaters. They enter areas exposed to the sun and protected from wind. The best spots generally lie on the north sides of lakes or impoundments since these areas receive the most exposure to the sun in spring and provide shelter from harsh north winds. Crappies follow minnows into the warming shallows as the baitfish seek the microscopic plankton that are beginning to bloom there.

In natural lakes, crappies hold near cover like reeds, dock pilings, brush, and remaining shallow weeds. In rivers and reservoirs, flooded brush, stumps, fallen trees, and fish attractors function similarly.

Stable weather draws crappies inshore and cold-front conditions drive them out. Regardless of precise location, knowing crappies are in the vicinity of shallow bays, backwaters, or cuts offers a starting place.

Lakes or reservoirs with shallow bays or cuts may host shallow crappie movements just after ice-out or just as the water begins to warm. When bodies of water lack such protected areas, however, several additional weeks may be needed for wind-exposed shallows to warm sufficiently to attract fish. In such lakes, most crappies usually remain suspended along the first drop-off-channel edge until the shallows warm enough to attract them.

As the water continues to warm toward 50°F, the environment grows more stable. Most crappies will generally be in an area from the extreme shallows out to the first drop-off, possibly shifting toward areas where they'll eventually spawn. These may or may not be the same areas they used earlier, depending on bottom content and cover.

Prespawn Period

Water Temperature: 50°F to Low 60°F Range
General Fish Mood: Neutral to Positive

Crappie activity begins near spawning areas. In reservoirs and rivers, these areas generally occur (1) where the bottom is sufficiently soft for crappies to sweep out a nest—generally sand-marl, but not mucky; (2) near some form of cover; (3) at the appropriate depth; (4) protected from wind.

In general, bays with timber, stumps, or brushpiles attract most crappies, rather than main-lake shorelines. Prime spots are from one to five feet deep.

Prespawn crappies congregate in these areas as the water rises toward 60°F. Males enter spawning areas first. Females may mill in and out, holding a bit deeper until spawning time. This is particularly true in natural lakes where crappies spawn in the shallows around reed or weed cover.

When crappies first enter spawning areas, they're spooky as they mill about in large groups. The longer they remain in the shallows, however, the more aggressive and territorial they become. Hormonal changes begin to trigger a darker color in males. In clear lakes, they can often be spotted as dark spots inside a tangled mass of reeds.

As waters warm, crappies become quite easy to catch on a variety of bobber presentations, particularly once males select spawning sites and begin sweeping nests.

Crappies enter shallow bays as waters warm into the 50°F range. Here they forage on huge schools of minnows, prior to moving to spawning arms.

Eventually, males attract females to the nest and spawning occurs.

All crappies in a body of water don't spawn at the same time, since all areas of a lake don't warm at the same pace. Expect spawning in the shallowest, most protected areas first, later in deeper or less protected areas that take longer to warm enough for spawning to begin.

Spawn Period

Water Temperature: Mid 60°F to Mid 70°F Range
General Fish Mood: Neutral

Spawning bouts between a male and female crappie may last hours. Females typically release eggs with several males over a week or so, longer if the process is interrupted by storms, wind, or cold fronts.

While crappies feed little during spawning, some fish strike at objects in the nest area. Since crappies tend to spawn in loose groups, some fish in an area may be spawning while others are in prespawn or postspawn.

Typical Spawning Months

AREA	MONTHS
Florida	March-April
Alabama-Georgia	March-April
Texas-Oklahoma	March-May
Kentucky-Tennessee	April-May
Missouri-Illinois-Iowa	April-June
Ohio	April-July
Oregon	March-June
Minnesota-Wisconsin	May-July
Ontario	June-August

In small waters, most crappie spawning generally occurs over a couple weeks. In large reservoirs, however, fish may have finished spawning in some areas, while they're preparing to spawn in others. Where good spawning areas are limited, crappies may use them in waves, with fish staging outside spawning areas until nesting sites are available. Eggs generally hatch in about a week, although males usually guard the fry until they disperse from the nest.

Eventually, when most spawning activity in an area has occurred, females begin filtering out of the shallows. Males remain behind, fanning the nest to oxygenate the eggs and provide fresh water, and to guard the nests from hungry predators.

Postspawn Period

Water Temperature: Mid 70°F Range
General Fish Mood: Negative to Neutral

Depending on the body of water and local weather conditions, crappies may take a week or two to recuperate from the rigors of spawning. Some don't survive, and fungus-infested fish are common in spawning channels as waters warm.

After leaving the nest, females filter across adjacent flats. Small groups of fish may linger around shallow cover like fish attractors or weed clumps. In general, however, they slowly move toward the nearest drop-off or developing weedline.

Crappies that move to drop-offs don't school tightly, though large aggregations of fish may occupy general areas. Crappies in deeper water may suspend from 5 to 15 feet below the surface, where they search for food.

Loose groups of crappies typically roam along channel edges and drop-offs, stopping occasionally at distinct features like weed clumps, underwater points, or channel bends.

Once hatchlings disperse, male crappies leave the nest and join the females, forming larger schools. Postspawn slowly blends into the Presummer Period.

Presummer Period

Water Temperature: 70°F Range
General Fish Mood: Neutral

Resumption of regular feeding patterns indicates the beginning of the Presummer Period, usually when water temperature reaches the mid 70°F range.

Presummer is a time of emerging weedgrowth and developing food chains. Feeding opportunities and patterns develop at different depths, and some crappies

Crappie Spawning Location In Reservoirs

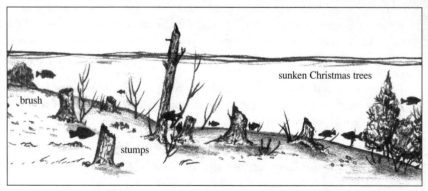

Crappies in reservoirs spawn around shallow cover like submerged brush and stumps. Complex structures hold larger groups of fish.

Deeper cover holds prespawn and postspawn fish. Cold fronts may also drive some fish from spawning areas into deeper cover. Sunken brushpiles and fish attractors like Christmas trees attract crappies, but they must be shallow to be used as spawning sites.

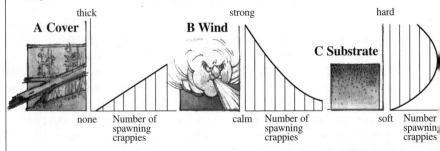

Crappie Spawning Conditions
Graphs show the best conditions for crappie spawning.

A Cover — thick / none — Number of spawning crappies

B Wind — strong / calm — Number of spawning crappies

C Substrate — hard / soft — Number spawning crappies

A. Crappies can spawn without cover, but thick cover draws large concentrations of fish. As a rule, cover is weeds in lakes and wood in reservoirs. Reservoirs with abundant vegetation function like lakes. Fallen trees are prime spawning sites for crappies.

B. Crappies spawn in calm areas, avoiding wind. They leave nests if strong winds arise.

C. Substrate of medium hardness is best. Crappies spawn on rock and stumps, but rarely. A muck or silt bottom is unsatisfactory because the male can't fan the eggs without smothering them.

D. Crappies can spawn in all but the muddiest water. They generally choose water clarity with 2- to 4-foot visibility, however. As a

may be caught on flats, along drop-offs, or suspended.

In general, however, crappies shift deeper during the Presummer Period. They move across shallow flats and perhaps use timber or weed clumps on deeper edges. In reservoirs, they roam channel edges and leave the backwaters in rivers for areas with a bit more current. Yet they may feed in many areas due to available prey—insects, larvae, minnows, fry.

Slowly, they move to the habitat they'll occupy during the upcoming Summer Period. In natural lakes and ponds, points and turns in the deep weededge draw increasingly more fish. In reservoirs, deeper timbered channel edges toward the mouths of coves collect schools of crappies. The extreme shallows become nearly devoid of crappies, while the drop-offs and confined open water outside the drop-offs host more fish.

Presummer is a time of transition, when a body of water transforms from the cooler-water environment of spring to the warmer-water environment of summer. Crappies begin to regroup and classic patterns begin to emerge.

Summer Peak Period

Water Temperature: Mid to Upper 70°F Range
General Fish Mood: Positive

During the Summer Peak, summer patterns move into high gear as schools of crappies set up on classic summer spots. Most of a lake's ecosystem reaches its maximum production during this period. The transformation from a cool to a warm environment is complete. Hatching insects fill the air, and rooted aquatic

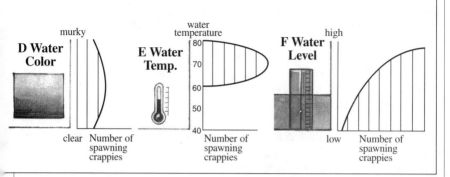

general rule, the clearer the water the deeper they spawn. Heavy cover like reeds or brush draw spawners shallow.

E. Crappies begin spawning when water temperature rises into the low 60°F range. Peak activity is around 70°F. Lakes and reservoirs don't warm uniformly, though, so spawning may continue for 6 weeks in a body of water.

F. A quick rise in water level when crappies are almost ready to spawn often causes a flurry of spawning activity. They take advantage of high water to spawn around inundated brush and grass. Falling water disrupts spawning, and in extreme cases, beds are left high and dry.

plants grow almost before one's eyes.

In natural lakes, distinct weedlines develop, and crappies roam their edges like race cars circling a track. In reservoirs, crappies gorge on shad along the edges of creek and river channels. They congregate in large schools, and fishing can be fast. This a great time to be on the water.

Basically then, a combination of environmental factors stimulates Summer Peak activity: (1) Crappies are hungry and aggressive; (2) schooling creates competitive activity; and (3) the water is alive and brimming with food.

Summer Period

Water Temperature: Annual Maximum Temperature
General Fish Mood: Negative to Positive

Summer arrives and with it hordes of mosquitoes and water skiers. Nature is in full gear, converting the sun's energy to living matter. Abundant prey in the form of fry, fingerlings, and insects are available. Crappies become more selective in their choice of meals. Consider factors like thermoclines, sunlight, increased metabolism, and competing species when testing fishing patterns.

Most larger crappies have left the shallows. During the Summer Period, they roam edges of cover, generally in the 12- to 22-foot range; the clearer the water, the deeper they'll usually be. Active fish may be on the edge of cover or slightly into it, while inactive fish often suspend outside cover.

In natural lakes, the best summer areas are deep cabbage or coontail weed-edges—particularly points and turns in those edges—and rock piles that rise slightly above the level of deepest sunlight penetration. Here, underwater plants or moss-covered rocks attract and hold the baitfish crappies prey on. Similar structure in strip pits, ponds, and impoundments also attracts crappies.

In most reservoirs, flooded timber, deep stumps, and manmade fish attractors substitute for natural weed cover, but patterns are similar. Crappies use the best wood along the edges of creek and river channels and select depths based on water clarity. Active fish hold in or next to cover, while fish suspended outside usually are moving or not aggressively feeding.

Crappies often suspend, particularly during daylight, and in clear water they feed primarily toward dusk and at night. Fishing the edges of cover around dawn and dusk often provides the best summertime catches. In dark-water lakes and reservoirs, crappies may feed during midday.

In summer, crappie activity occurs deeper than in spring, although fish remain above the thermocline. They roam confined open water near cover, holding at a suitable depth based on water clarity. Twilight or cloudy weather may draw them shallower.

Postsummer Period

Water Temperature: *Rapidly Cooling From Annual Maximum*
General Fish Mood: *Neutral to Positive*

The Postsummer Period is a reversal of the Presummer process, occurring at the end of summer when waters cool. Hot days with dead-calm periods followed by cool nights are typical. Days grow shorter, sending a signal to the ecosystem that life is slowing down.

Most of the food in lakes, rivers, and reservoirs has already been produced, so predation reduces food supplies. Weeds thin, insect hatches dwindle, and water levels in rivers often are low, forcing fish into deep holes.

Crappies generally respond to their changing environment by holding tighter to cover and showing less tendency to suspend. Fish a weedline or timberline and you

Crappies are most active in the shallows during the spring Cold-water, Prespawn, and Spawn Periods, although some crappies may also be shallow during fall.

66

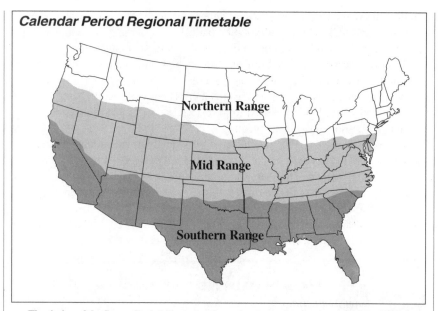

Calendar Period Regional Timetable

Northern Range

Mid Range

Southern Range

The timing of the Spawn Period illustrates the region-by-region progression of the Calendar Periods. Region (latitude), water temperature, weather trends, length of daylight, and competition for habitat are just a few of the factors that influence spawning time. But not all crappies spawn at the same time even in the same body of water. While most adult fish in a lake may spawn during a few days of ideal conditions, some spawn earlier and some later..

Regionally, crappie spawning may begin in early March in the South or as late as mid-July in southern Canada. The following chart illustrates typical spawning months for crappies in representative areas:

may not spot a suspended fish on sonar, but it's also possible to catch a bunch of crappies by casting a jig into timber or weeds. It's necessary to fish 'em to find 'em, rather than locating them with a depthfinder.

Crappies concentrated on deep edges of cover makes them easier to find and catch. Often you can catch a bunch from a school and return in several days for similar success.

Turnover Period

Water Temperature: *Upper 50°F to low 50°F Range*
General Fish Mood: *Negative*

Shallow bodies of water stirred by wind or those with substantial current don't stratify and therefore don't turn over. Yet the transition from a warm to a cold environment requires adjustment.

In stratified waters, thermoclines usually remain intact through the end of the Postsummer Period. Cold winds and rain chill the surface of the water quickly. The shrinking thermocline ruptures, and mixing continues until the entire body of water top to bottom has the same temperature and oxygen content.

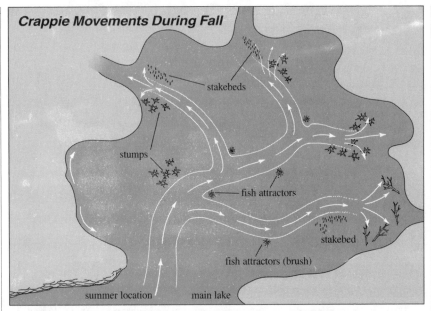

Crappie Movements During Fall

stakebeds

stumps

fish attractors

stakebed

fish attractors (brush)

summer location   main lake

   Fall migrations begin after the first cold front in September. After leaving the main channel, crappies follow the same routes they used in spring. Their first stop or staging area is a pocket of stumps; middepth fish attractors; an old roadbed; or the junction of a creek, slough, or ditch. They remain in these areas until cooler temperatures push them shallower into brushpiles, downed timber, grassbeds, and shoreline vegetation that isn't left dry by falling water levels.

   Fish attractors placed along migration routes pay greater dividends during fall than during any other season. Stakebeds are particularly effective, although any kind of attractor will hold fish because cover is at a premium during fall and winter drawdowns. Note the location of the fish attractors—sites for crappies when they're properly built and anchored.

   In fall, because of the water clarity, cast jigs on ultralight gear or work them under a slip cork on spincast tackle for spooky crappies.

   Most reservoirs draw down their water level in winter, which leaves cover dry that was underwater in spring and summer.

At times, stagnant bottom water gives off a sulfurous odor as it rises to the surface, and dead weeds and other bottom debris may float on the surface or wash ashore.

Fishing during the Turnover Period on stratified waters is difficult. Since all bodies of water don't turn over at the same time, however, switch to waters that already have turned over, waters that haven't yet turned over, or waters that don't stratify.

The behavior of crappies during turnover is unknown. They may be bothered by unstable conditions, so the best fishing usually occurs in shallow areas least affected by turnover, such as current areas or bays attached to the lake with a small channel.

Under these conditions, seek the best available cover in shallow water. While you probably won't get into numbers of fish, a few stragglers could save the day. Areas with weeds or wood are good choices.

Coldwater Period (Fall)

Water Temperature: Low 50°F Range to Annual Minimum
General Fish Mood: Neutral to Positive

The Coldwater Period runs from the end of the Turnover Period to freeze-up or to the coldest water of the year on bodies of water that don't freeze. It's a gradual slowing down and stabilization of the entire ecosystem, and crappie metabolism slows in response to the cooling water.

In many cases, turnover has opened the door to deeper, formerly unusable areas below the thermocline during summer. Now crappies can shift into deeper reoxygenated water.

Soon after turnover in natural lakes, they may hold near deep edges of healthy weedbeds, particularly if structural elements aren't available in deeper water. Sometimes they suspend in open water of bays. Deeper rocky points and sunken islands also attract crappies during this period.

In reservoirs, crappies begin schooling in deep (15- to 30-foot) creek channel bends with wood cover. On large rivers, they leave current areas for deep 5- to 15-foot backwaters or connected natural lakes. Huge schools form by late fall. In small rivers without deep backwaters, crappies move into deeper pools as water levels drop.

In all cases, they tend to suspend near the surface less. They may suspend, but usually within 5 or 10 feet of the bottom. They sometimes hold on the bottom, becoming hard to distinguish on sonar until they become active and move off bottom.

The stable Coldwater Period is prime time for crappie angling. Schooling concentrates fish in distinct areas, and once you locate them, you can enjoy action regularly by using slow bottom-oriented presentations.

In the Coldwater Period, big crappies often school near structural elements such as brush piles near creek channels.

Winter or Frozen Water Period

Water Temperature: Annual Minimum for an Extended Period
General Fish Mood: Neutral

Winter or Frozen Water is the longest period of the year in northern waters where ice may cover lakes for up to five months. In southern waters, the temperature may not drop below 40°F, sometimes dipping below 50°F in southern lakes like Okeechobee in Florida.

Crappies feed on small prey through the Winter Period and can provide excellent ice fishing. In the South, open-water angling can be good, too, though few anglers pursue crappies at this time of year. Fishing small jigs 30 feet deep from a boat in the face of wind and rain or sleet is too much discomfort for most folks. Fishing from a toasty fish house over prime structure is easier and more comfortable.

In general, crappies occupy the same types of areas they use during the Fall Coldwater Period. Deep edges of cover (weeds or timber), channel edges, and rocky humps produce fish. The best areas usually lie in less than 30 feet of water and seldom are as deep as 40 feet. In small lakes, ponds, or bays, they may suspend over the main-lake basin.

As in the Coldwater Period, most early and midwinter crappie activity occurs within 5 or 10 feet of bottom. Later in the period, as ice cover thins or the water begins to warm, crappies begin to suspend nearer the surface.

Most crappie activity in winter occurs during the low-light periods of dawn and dusk or at night, unless water color is very dark. Anglers night fishing from fish houses note that crappies are attracted to the lighted area beneath their holes, just as they're drawn to the glow of lanterns hung below bridges in spring. Night fishing can be surprisingly productive during winter.

Crappies are concentrated and catchable on small lures and livebait presented slowly at or slightly above their depth level. Use sonar to determine the depth crappies are using. Then experiment with combinations of tiny ice flies, spoons, and jigs tipped with minnows or insect larvae.

In the North, as many crappies are caught through ice as from open water.

YEAR OF THE CHANNEL CATFISH

Secrets to Seasonal Periods of Response

Calendar Periods categorize behavior, location, activity, and catchability. The annual rhythm of rivers differs from that of lakes, and channel catfish activity differs from other species. The growth and death of aquatic vegetation is a major influence in lakes and reservoirs. Rivers, on the other hand, experience turbulent run-off. Most importantly, catfish spawn much later than most fish.

A long Prespawn Period produces extended good fishing. Catfishing begins after rivers stabilize during spring and catfish move into a long Prespawn Period. After spawning, cats settle into holding areas for the summer. Fall cool water and rain generally moves cats down-river to large deep holes where they spend winter. Winter, which may include ice cover, reduces catfish activity, except during periods of extended warm weather.

The catfish calendar includes the 10 In-Fisherman Calendar Periods, beginning with the Winter Period. Our Spring Period includes the end of the Spring Cold Water Period, plus Prespawn, Postspawn, and Pre-summer—spawning periods lasting well into June and July.

Our Summer Period includes Summer Peak, Summer, and Postsummer periods. The Cooling Period moves into the Cold-water Period preceding Winter.

Winter or Frozen Water Period

Water Temperature: Coldest Water for an Extended Period
General Fish Mood: Negative

This extended period can't be defined by precise environmental markers since channel catfish are found in a variety of geographic areas. The Winter Period includes two In-Fisherman Calendar Periods: Coldwater and Frozen Water or Winter. In the southern half of the catfish range, ice-up doesn't occur.

The Winter Period is characterized by almost constant cold temperatures. How cold depends on geographic location and the severity of the winter. In Minnesota

While catfish can be caught in some bodies of water all year long, most cats become lethargic during winter.

and Manitoba, water on lakes and parts of most rivers is under 3 feet of ice. Water temperatures in winter range from about 32°F to 39°F. In southern states, water temperatures usually are in the 40°F range, 50°F in Florida.

We define this period by catfish activity, which is basically the same no matter where they're located. In winter, catfish face a long period of temperatures much colder than during the rest of the year. They go into a winter lethargy, a sort of suspended animation as they lie in the deepest holes or deepest pockets off the main current flow, areas with slow-flowing water. In small rivers, a holding hole might be 6 feet deep or less. In bigger rivers, holes may be 20 to 40 feet deep.

Scuba divers report seeing catfish behind boulders that break current. Where enough boulders aren't available, catfish appear to snug behind anything that reduces current. To reduce water resistance, other catfish then line up behind the first one, nose to tail in a chainlike formation.

In the middle and southern regions of the country, catfish don't completely stop moving and feeding during winter. A radio tagging study on the Missouri River showed catfish almost completely dormant during a bitterly cold winter.

1 Prespawn	2 Spawn	3 Postspawn	4 Presummer	5 Summer Peak	6 Summer	7 Postsummer	8 Turnover	9 Coldwater	10 Winter

But during a mild winter, they moved short distances. An extended period of warm weather in January or February may stimulate catfish activity near deeper river holes that are easy to locate because the water's usually low. Since fish are highly concentrated in predictable locations, tremendous catches are possible.

During midwinter when cats are stacked and inactive in river holes, it's often possible to snag them by vertical jigging. This is illegal, however, in most areas.

Spring Coldwater Period

Water Temperature: Rising
General Fish Mood: Neutral to Positive

When ice leaves or early spring weather arrives, walleyes, pike, and sauger move quickly through the Prespawn Period and into the Spawn Period. It's a time of rapid transition. Not so with channel catfish that probably won't spawn for months, even in far northern waters where the Prespawn-Spawn transition is compressed.

In rivers, early spring usually means continued cold and turbid water. Northern areas experience snow melt and cold spring rains. Southern areas receive cold spring rains. As the water begins to warm gradually, catfish activity increases.

In early spring, catfish might still spend most of their time in deep holes. Eventually, rising water temperatures stimulate catfish metabolism. No distinct temperature marks this point. In southern regions, where water temperatures have been in the 50s, catfish might start feeding when water temperatures reach the low 60°F range. In northern regions, 45°F usually means cats will prowl, but temperatures in the upper 50°F range are better.

Prespawn migration usually continues until catfish reach a dam. They may use the tailwater area for foraging and may also spawn there. More likely, though, they eventually drift back downstream to appropriate spawning sites.

Mostly, we sense when the first good run of cats will begin aggressively feeding. Spring weather will have whipsawed from nasty to nice, but suddenly the weather's nice for days in a row. A spring thundershower scents the air, and as you walk across your lawn, it bounces with a give in the soil. The ground is about to come alive at night with the first nightcrawlers. Trees are budding; frogs are beginning their evening chorus; and ducks, geese, grouse, and most of the rest of the animal world are active.

Catfish are moving, but still avoiding direct current. And current is stronger now than during any other time of year. Fish are concentrated in areas of reduced current—the core of a hole, the deepest spot, but more likely shoreline holding areas.

This is the season for live baits or sour baits. Cats can find plenty of fish that have died over winter and are beginning to decompose as water temperatures rise.

Prespawn Period

Water Conditions: Rising Temperatures and Stabilizing River Flows
General Fish Mood: Positive

What river walleyes do in fall, channel catfish do in spring. They move, usually upstream, sometimes into smaller feeder rivers, searching first for food and second for spawning habitat.

No sharp demarcation is present between the preceding period and this one. They blend naturally as water temperatures continue to rise into the 60°F range and river flows stabilize. The main difference is catfish behavior. Their metabolic rate is much higher, so they need more food and are better able to search for it. Higher water also offers a variety of areas.

Typical Spawning Months

AREA	MONTHS
Florida	April-early June
Alabama-Georgia	May-June
Texas-Oklahoma	May-June
Kentucky-Tennessee	June-July
Missouri-Illinois-Iowa	June-July
Ohio	June-early August
Minnesota-Wisconsin	June-early August
Manitoba	July-August

The earliest upriver movements are motivated more by the need to feed than by a spawning urge.

Because more areas are available than earlier in the year, cats no longer must accept the limited forage in holes where they spent the winter.

Barriers such as big dams and low-head dams temporarily concentrate cats. This period compares somewhat to the prespawn movement of steelhead in rivers, with fish constantly moving, stopping to hold in spots offering food and protection from current, then moving again to better feeding opportunities.

Catch a fish or two from a small spot and return in a day or two and catch three more. The spot is restocked by the restless movement of the fish.

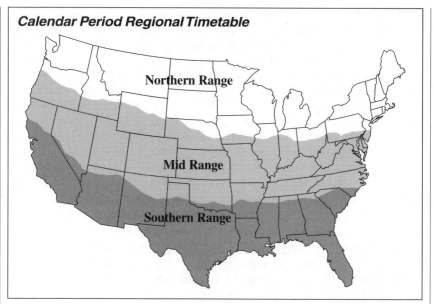

Calendar Period Regional Timetable

Northern Range

Mid Range

Southern Range

The timing of the channel catfish Spawn Period illustrates the region-by-region progression of the Calendar Periods. Region (latitude), water temperature, weather trends, length of daylight, and competition for habitat are just a few of the factors influencing the exact timing of the spawn. Remember, not all channel cats spawn at the same time even in the same body of water. While the bulk of the adult fish on a given river may spawn during a few days of ideal conditions, some still spawn early and some late. Regionally, the onset of channel catfish spawning may begin in early May in the South and as late as August in southern Canada.

In high water without impassable barriers, catfish may move 75 miles or more—channel cats have moved as far as 111 miles in 36 days. So long as the water's high and fish are finding food, they keep moving. At times, however, they move only a few miles.

Where catfish spawn is determined by their location when spawning time nears. Apparently cats don't always return to the same spawning locations, although this hasn't been verified. They do return to general areas, however. Many catfish in the lower portion of the Red River in Manitoba, for example, return to the same slough off the main river each year, despite varying water levels. Catfish move upstream, looking for food and future spawning sites.

Prespawn movement often continues until cats reach an impassable barrier like a dam. They search the area for possible spawning locations like holes in riprap or rocky outcroppings near the dam. If the area below the dam is too silty, they drift downstream to look for spawning sites. Spawners may spread over a long stretch of river.

The Prespawn Period offers potential for the year's best fishing. Fish are moving—searching and actively feeding. Be there.

Spawn Period

Water Temperatures: 75°F or Higher
General Fish Mood: Positive-Negative

Catfish spawning may span a month or more, so the spawn doesn't negatively affect angling as it would if all cats spawned at the same time. Also, channel cats bite almost anything near a spawning hole, so find a spawning area and you may find good fishing.

The spawn is triggered by the length of daylight (photoperiod), cats sense in the brain, probably in the pineal gland. Linking spawning in part to length of daylight is one guarantee against eggs hatching too early or too late, which could happen if spawning time were based solely on water temperature. In addition, an internal biological clock causes eggs to mature even with external stimuli absent.

Catfish are motivated to spawn by water temperatures of 75°F or above. According to some studies, temperatures approaching 80°F are ideal. Catfish kept in water too cool for spawning will spawn when water temperatures quickly rise to 75°F, if time of year is appropriate. Spawning, then, is regulated by the interplay of an internal clock, length of daylight, and water temperature.

Channel Cat Growth Rates

	Average Length at Age (inches)								
Location	1	3	5	7	9	11	13	15	17
Red River, Manitoba	10	11	15	20	20	27	27	33	34
Several Kansas Lakes	3	10	13	17	19				
Salt River, MO	3	8	12	16					
Oklahoma Average	4	12	16	20	24	25	26		
Des Moines River, IA	2	8	12	17	21	25	27		
Lake Moultrie, SC	3	11	17	24	29	32	36		
Kentucky Lake, TN	4	9	12	17	22				
Lake Havasu, CA	3	7	9	14	18	19	23		
Lake Erie	3	9	12	14					
Potomac River, MD	8	13	18						
Wisconsin River, WI	5	9	12	16	19	22	24	27	
Missouri River, NE	2	9	13	17	16				
Lake Oahe, SD	1	8	13	17	20	22	24	24	25
Pony Express Lake, MO	4	13	18	22	24	26	25		
Mississippi River, IA	5	12	16	20	23				
St. Lawrence River, PQ	4	8	10	12	13	14	16	17	

Channel catfish growth rate has been studied throughout their range. Cats lack scales, the structure most commonly used for determining age, but pectoral and dorsal spines and vertebrae are sectioned and examined microscopically. Year marks (annuli) are counted and measured to determine age and growth rate. This table describes average growth rates for various populations. Note the growth variability and the many years required for a cat to reach trophy size. Cats, like many fish, probably grow most during the period from late spring through midsummer. Population growth rates are determined by abundance and type of forage, quality of habitat (including water), length of growing season, and competition for food. The oldest channel cat on record was a specimen about 40 years old from the St. Lawrence River. The oldest fish grow little and age determination isn't precise.

The Catfish Calendar

1. Prespawn
2. Spawn
3. Postspawn
4. Presummer
5. Summer Peak
6. Summer
7. Postsummer
8. Fall Turnover
9. Coldwater
10. Winter*1,2,3,4,5
   potential extensive
   overlap of periods.

*The coldest water of the year.

Gregorian Calendar	Jan	Feb	Mar	Apr	May	June	July	Aug	Sept	Oct	Nov	Dec
Northern Range	10			9	1	2,3,4,5		6	7	9	10	
Mid Range	10	9	1		2, 3, 4, 5			6		7	9	10
Southern Range	10	9	1			2, 3, 4, 5			6		7	9	10

The 10 Calendar Periods of fish response varies in length from year to year. Unusually warm or cool weather affects the length of the periods. They can vary as much as 4 weeks from one year to the next. The periods aren't based on the Gregorian calendar, so they don't occur on specific dates each year. Instead, the Calendar Periods are based on nature's clock.

In addition, Calendar Periods vary by regions of the country. The rivers of the South experience an extended Summer Period and a brief Winter Period. In contrast, rivers along the U.S.-Canadian border have extended Coldwater and Winter Periods. Channel cats in Florida or Texas could be in the Spawning Period while those in northern Minnesota are still in the Winter Period.

Unusual about the channel catfish calendar is the long period during which individual cats in a population may be in one of 6 different periods. In most situations, this doesn't affect fish location and fishing patterns.

Spawning can take place as early as May in the South and August in the North. In Missouri, dates range from late May to early July. The most common spawning month across the channel cat's geographic range is June.

To begin the spawn, a male channel cat seeks a hole or pocket in a bank. Catfish in ponds with no suitable spawning locations don't spawn. If artificial spawning structures are added, they may spawn.

The spawning hole should be secure, preferably with only one entrance big enough to admit the male and female. A small entrance not much larger than a fish's body is ideal. Big fish spawn in big holes, small fish in small holes. If the hole's entrance isn't much bigger than the male, he lies with his head toward the entrance, nearly filling it, to effectively guard eggs and fry.

In small rivers, crevices near rocky riffles offer possible spots for spawning holes. Undercut banks, muskrat holes, and objects in the water—hollow logs, car bodies, tires, buckets—are possible spawning sites.

First, the male sweeps the hole to clean and enlarge it. Eventually he lures a

Stable summer weather means consistent fishing as cats settle into predictable locations and feeding patterns.

female into the hole. The female ejects a gelatinous clump of eggs, from 2,000 to over 70,000, depending on the size of the fish, and the male fertilizes them. Then the female leaves or is driven from the hole by the male. She produces one clutch of eggs a year. Males, however, may spawn more than once if the spawning season is extended. The supply of available males often exceeds the number of sexually mature females.

The male is a good guardian. As mentioned, his massive head usually fills the entrance to the nest. He's aggressive in his defense of the eggs. Anything stuck near him will be hit or bit. Holes with two or more entrances probably suffer egg loss because the male can't guard them as well. The male also aerates and keeps silt off the eggs by fanning them with his fins.

Little is known about what happens next in the wild, because observations are based on catfish in clear hatchery ponds where they may behave differently. But we do know that eggs hatch in about a week. Then fry spend about a week in the nest being protected by the male before they enter the river and begin life among predators.

Some observers say the young slip into the river and are immediately on their own. Others, who observed cats in small ponds, report that males protect fry for several days after they leave the nest. Survival of the young is probably better in turbid water than in clear water, because reduced visibility in turbid water conceals the young from many predators.

Settling Period
(Includes Postspawn and Presummer Periods)
Water Temperature Range: *Upper 70°F to Mid 80°F*
General Fish Mood: *Neutral to Positive*

This period, important in fishing for some fish, isn't vital to catfishermen because the catfish spawning period is so extended. Even in ponds where water temperatures and length of daylight are identical for all fish, not all catfish spawn at the same time.

Catfish probably go through a type of recuperative period after spawning, but to an angler, it doesn't matter if a few fish are recuperating because at any given time, some fish are almost always feeding.

This period probably occurs in late June to July in much of the catfish range. Catfish are on the move again, often moving downstream from spawning sites, looking for deep cover-laden holes that offer security and food. Downstream movement isn't automatic. If the spawning area offers good summer habitat, they may linger.

If water levels are high and rising, channel cats move either upstream or downstream during this settling period. More typically, though, water levels are dropping, so they move downstream, often leaving small tributaries to enter bigger rivers. These movements are more pronounced in small creeks than in big rivers.

Summer Period

(Includes Summer Peak, Summer, and Postsummer Periods)
Water Temperatures: *Annual Maximum 80°F and Above*
General Fish Mood: *Positive*

The Summer Period includes much of July, August, and September in most of the channel cat's range. Summer offers prime fishing. Fish are in predictable locations. They feed aggressively, although not all the time. Plenty of food is available, at least during the beginning of summer, so they add much of their year's growth during this period that doesn't end until water begins to cool during fall. Find the best holes with the biggest catfish and fish them with the right baits at the right time.

During most seasons, channel cats in rivers prefer to hold near cover in deeper holes or river pools.

Cooling Period

(Includes the Turnover and Fall Coldwater Periods)
Water Temperatures: *Cooling from 80°F*
General Fish Attitude: *Positive to Neutral to Negative*

As late summer slips into fall, longer cooler nights and cool rains lower river temperatures. In early fall, catfish location depends mostly on river level. During stable levels, catfish continue holding in holes where they spent the summer. Heavy rain during September or October may pull catfish upriver. Generally, though, especially when water temperatures begin to cool into the 60°F range, cats move downstream toward bigger, deeper water and deep wintering holes.

Eventually, the biggest, deepest holes concentrate large groups of catfish. As water temperatures continue to fall, catfish activity is confined to the immediate vicinity of the wintering hole. Catfish location can mean good fishing now. Obviously though, it's important to fish the right holes.

Periods of stable warm weather also produce periods of fine catfishing during fall, once holding areas are found.